I Am My Own Sanctuary

"If you want to read a book about taking good care of yourself that is approachable, honest, wise, and funny, then read this one. It's an enticing, educating, encouraging, and entertaining read. Actually, all those adjectives describe Meggie, too!"

David Hayward (AKA the NakedPastor)
Author, Cartoonist, and Life Coach

"This book is full of highly valuable and practical information to help you find, embody and live out your vocational calling. Jesus said, 'The meek inherit the earth.' I believe this means those of us who are willing to be vulnerable have the most influence. Meggie created a book that finally pulls off the 'Christian' mask and vulnerably shares real-life lessons from her path in ministry. The good, the bad, the beautiful, the ugly, the funny, All of it. This book is a must-read for anyone looking to find their calling and path in this life or the church. I believe this book serves as the unspoken, highly desired bridge to living out everyday life in a powerful way as a modern day Christian."

Aj Amyx
Life and Business Coach, ajAmyx.com

"An honest take on how a young woman finds herself through the rigidity of religion and somehow through it all discovering her own sanctuary, finding inner happiness and a true sense of self."

Maria Henderson
Author of **The Boss Mom Mentality**

"There are many elements that make *I Am My Own Sanctuary* an addicting read. Meggie invites you first, to be her friend. As your friendship develops with her as you turn each page, you find that even if you have different life experiences from her, that she still wants you to question, reflect, and grow into your own self. Meggie wants you to laugh, she wants you to dig deep, and she wants you to make room in yourself for holiness—not for strict rules or religion or the voices of others. As you turn the pages, you'll find that Meggie is a gifted teacher—a ready mentor—and someone who's suggested reading list will quickly fill up your bookshelf. If you're at a point in your faith where you're asking yourself for another perspective, you've found the book that'll help you refine your own."

Miranda Priddy
Co-host of the Listening Chair Podcast

"As soon as I began reading Meggie's new book, I had an immediate thought...This book 'feels' exactly right. The more that I read, the more that my feeling was strongly confirmed. If I'm being completely honest, this book had me at the title itself: *I Am My Own Sanctuary*. Speaking of 'sanctuary,' why do so many make an effort to visit that place each week? You know what I'm referring to right? The sanctuary is that special place in church buildings where all the magic happens. I suppose it's because the sanctuary is the place where we understand that God fully dwells. Here's a news flash, however. Every building and room previously labeled a 'sanctuary' was but a shadow of the real one. The *real* sanctuary is *me*. However, 'me' can only be understood in the first person. This is also true of the divine as well. According to Psalm 46:10, (Be still and know that I AM God) true knowledge of the divine can only be found in the place of stillness and in the place of I AM. Stillness is the place where we come home to ourselves and understand the ultimate phrase of consciousness and awareness...'I AM.'

If 'me' is the place where we truly recognize the dwelling of 'I AM' (sanctuary), it's imperative that we 'return to church' by coming home to ourselves. Meggie's book is a courageous memoir of her journey out of a rigid form of evangelical Christianity and back home to her true sanctuary of self. This book will have you laughing hysterically, and moments later, releasing your own tears of empathy and sadness. Let me encourage you to read her book and discover that you too are your own truest sanctuary."

Jamal Jivanjee
Bestselling Author, Podcaster, and Life Coach

"Meggie has a special way with storytelling that not only promotes deep conversations that we need to have with ourselves and others, but does so while we're wiping tears of laughter from our eyes! My heart needed this book, and my list of people to share it with grew with each page!"

Ashley Boyd
Author and Life Coach at AnointedWithPurpose.com

"Meggie opens up about what it is really like to be a Christian. She gives insight to not only life in the church, but the experiences she has had throughout her life. Each page brings out a new story that will make you laugh and give you some questions to ponder. She encourages you to find your inner holiness and to make yourself your own sanctuary. If you are looking for a book to make you laugh but also help you work through hard questions of faith, this is the book for you."

Carly Redding
Token 18-Year-Old

First Edition

Cover design and layout by Rafael Polendo (polendo.net)
Author photo by Paul Shakelford

Unless otherwise identified, all Scripture quotations in this publication are taken from the Holy Bible, New International Version®, NIV®. Copyright ©1973, 1978, 1984, 2011 by Biblica, Inc.™ Used by permission of Zondervan. All rights reserved worldwide. www.zondervan.com The "NIV" and "New International Version" are trademarks registered in the United States Patent and Trademark Office by Biblica, Inc.™

ISBN 978-1-938480-49-2

This volume is printed on acid free paper and meets ANSI Z39.48 standards.

Printed in the United States of America

 QUOIR

Published by Quoir
Orange, California

www.quoir.com

I AM MY OWN SANCTUARY

HOW A RECOVERING HOLY-ROLLER FOUND HEALING AND POWER

MEGGIE LEE CALVIN

Dedication

To my grandparents, Brenda and Guy,
who first taught me to recognize the Holy within.

Acknowledgements

Thank you to Brittany Donals and York Moon for
being the test readers of this odd beast of a book
and assuring the proper landage of jokes.

Thank you to Anna Rhea and Aj Amyx for assuring
that the landing was a grammatical one.

Thank you to Jamal Jivanjee for suggesting that
this book land in the library of Quoir Publishing,
and with it, me into the Quoir family.

Thank you to Rafael and Teighlor Polendo for
making a safe place to land for spiritually-attuned
content-creators that disrupt thought patterns.

And last, but not least, thank you to Garrett and Henley
for letting me land the role of a lifetime as their family
member and for supporting, "write-night Tuesday."

Ego Sanctuario Meo

(I Am My Own Sanctuary)

Table of Contents

Introduction

Hi, I'm Meg and I'm a recovering holly-roller.

(Hi, Meg.)

I used to believe that I *had* to read the Bible every day.

I used to believe that love from God, like love from others, was performance-based.

I used to believe that church services were a mandatory part of life.

I used to believe that being Christian meant that you didn't befriend those of other faiths.

I used to believe that being a Christian meant only listening to Christian music.

I used to believe that God would only love me if I were a virgin, so I was until my husband.

I used to be utterly afraid of my body, afraid of my sexuality.

I used to slut-shame those who were not afraid of theirs.

I used to think that I was weak in my faith if I felt anger or any other "unattractive" emotion.

I used to look down on those who cussed, drank and smoked.

I used to make *every* decision based on the opinions of my church members.

I used not to know about the mind, body, soul, and spirit connection as it was not taught in my religious upbringing.

I used not to be aware of my own power, my own worth.

Over the past 7 years, that's all changed.

In the following pages of this book, I vulnerably share how I've overcome being a burnt out, overworked holly-roller and now have confidence, peace and certainty in who I was made to be and the work that I was made to do.

As result, I now have published two books, have a marriage that is on fire, love hanging out with my daughter, host a top podcast and get paid as a speaker. All of this has been possible because I chose to get outside of *all* my limiting beliefs of how a woman of God should be and started questioning *everything*.

Now...enough of all the seriousness. Let's have some fun and dive into this book.

Be wary of your next tattoo idea. Because it might, in all actuality, be a book idea that will require a *much* higher pain tolerance.

I have always been obsessed with grit. This ability to bounce back after adversity and keep on towards a goal demands my committed curiosity.

Why is it that some get going when the going gets tough and others don't? Why do some burnout too soon, while others cross the figurative finish-line?

The furthest thing from athletic, my favorite thing to do while being forced into watching any sport is to psychoanalyze the athletes before they shoot the ball or run the bases for a touchdown. Oh, yes, Super Bowl meetings. I mean...functions? Gatherings? Parties? Yes, there it is, "parties." (See, I know sports stuff.)

I irritate the poor soul who squished in on the couch next to me, by constantly blurting out things like, "What do you think number fourteen is visualizing right now? Is he doing a deep breathing exercise? Is it just me, or is it too loud? How exactly is he to analyze his next move with all of that shouting and clapping? I mean the guy can't even hear the mantra that he and his sports psychologists made up together. Can everyone *please* just be quiet for a sec so number fourteen can focus?!"

And then there are those athletes like Ryan Shazier who have been through hell and back, yet remain kind and unshakable. Isn't this mind-blowing? These types always leave me a little star struck, as if I have encountered a mutant X-man of sorts who have some rare superpower of resiliency. He has every reason in the world to be angry, vengeful and to no longer give a flip, but with great grit and grace, he forges onward.

As the poet, Naomi Shihab Nye writes,

"Before you know kindness as the deepest
thing inside, you must know sorrow as the other deepest thing.
You must wake up with sorrow.
You must speak it 'til your voice
Catches the thread of all sorrows and
You see the size of the cloth.

Then it is only kindness that makes sense anymore,
Only kindness that ties your shoes
And sends you out into the day to
mail letters and purchase bread,
Only kindness that raises its head
From the crowd of the world to say
It is I you have been looking for,
and then goes with you everywhere
Like a shadow or a friend."

My great-grandmother, Ola Lee, encompassed this poem. As a Hellenistic southern belle, mighty tales of this matriarch were shared like the parting of the Red Sea to the Israelites. Her legend kept us grounded in God and grounded in our own potential. Being born the youngest after three older (Rose bowl-playin') brothers, her snort-like sounds as an infant earned her the nickname "pig." The name stuck, and she became known as "momma pig" by *everyone* forever more. (Seriously—it's on her tombstone.)

Although her own mother was the *furthest* thing from a self-less and kind role model (She was *very* precarious), Momma Pig rose above the ashes as exactly that. She displayed physical grit on her dairy farm and emotional grit through infidelity and divorce. Her divorce not only lost her everything, including the farm, but it was during that time that she gained another mouth to feed when she adopted her nephew after her sister's passing. Intellectual grit was also exuded as she then went back to school in her late-forties and became a nurse at the state mental hospital. Through great grit, her goals of professional and financial success were *all* achieved, and she altruistically shared their fruit with her family.

It was necessary to hear encouraging stories like hers as our family figured out life together. There was divorce, war, and other equally fun external factors that established grit within us at an early age. Even as a kid, I was fully aware that my parents were *earnestly* working against the cards that had been dealt to them.

I picture a younger version of my Mom escaping an unhealthy marriage with my biological dad. I see her in her 30s where she forged through international airports, the four of us on toddler leashes (Don't judge. We weren't the best of listeners.), mounds of luggage in tow from tarmac to terminal as the Army shipped my stepdad (and only dad) around. "Isn't this a fun adventure, everyone?" she would say with nervous confidence.

Before my dad was the mighty military man of my childhood, he was a young boy who fled Mexico on a raft with his family. Once in the States and in the throes of generational poverty, his dad struggled with alcoholism and there were moments of abuse. Even in these darker days, they lived from a place of grit and *never* went on welfare.

My dad found himself in an English-speaking classroom unable to understand the language or the people. Despite this, he kept his grades high and became the fastest runner in the school. However, due to the costs, he was unable to join the track team. And if being in poverty wasn't enough to make school tough, the other kids weren't always kind. The scars of white kids throwing rocks at him still remain on his face, that face that has seen some *shit*.

Both of my parents, in different ways, successfully rose above their challenges. But their battles, as they do in all relational systems, inherently became mine. As Dr. Murray Bowen teaches in his Family Systems Theory—more to come on this—parents pass on their anxieties to their kids; and while there have been palpable doses of grace poured over my family, remnants of these inherited worries remain *and* along with them—the desire to overcome them.

I guess I come by my obsession of grit naturally, for my family is *unstoppably* irrepressible.

As Bowen's Family Systems Theory also teaches, our relational patterns within our childhood homes, follow us into our careers. My obsession with grit soon took on its current shape of sustainable servant leadership. This was a good fit for me because I came out of the womb addicted to the rush of playing tag with my goals, and since I served in the ministry, my workaholic nature was commended. My first sermon gets the credit for initiating this ridiculously long round of chase. The topic was on "counting your blessings," and I was the mature age of thirteen. It was poorly and exegetically built on Proverbs 17:22. My benediction was Bing Crosby's song from *White Christmas*, "Count Your Blessings." And yes, I *did* sing it. The high that I felt from writing and presenting it apparently affected the church leaders who were encouraged to add me to the payroll just a short four years later.

You guessed it; I was "special." Ya know, one of those odd middle schoolers whose social life *is* the church. (Whack-job alert!) I initially enjoyed the constant affirmation I felt as I sang or spoke. In time, as I matured, this community of faith led me into an authentic relationship with the healing Christ.

What once met an adolescent need fostered my vocational calling.

As I write this, I have been on a church staff for fifteen years. Yep—you know those years where most twenty-somethings explore other gigs, take gap years and have all sorts of regrettable fun? Not for this gal. For better or for worse, I have served in the non-profit/religious sector since I was a teen, and this, my friends, takes grit. No pity-card here, just callin' it like I see it.

I think I also picked up on a need for grit in ministry because I saw so many ministerial leaders who were on the verge of professional/spiritual burn out or charred to a crisp by their parishioners.

In my experience, some of the loudest voices in churches seem to come from those who are not only the *most* emotionally broken, but are also the *least* interested in being healed. And what do we do with them? We recruit them to chair committees. Yep, and rather than dealing with their own darkness, as life coach, Aj Amyx says, "they hide behind the scriptures and find edification and self-esteem by tearing others down" through their micro-managing ways of advent banners and lengths of prayers in worship.

Of course, this is me judging them from my own place of hurt (and we're going to unpack difficult relationships later on), but that is how I felt. Ya know what I mean? And, I hear ya, Dear Reader Friend, I know God's grace covers all and that Jesus hung out with lepers and tax collectors, *but* do I really have to sit through another hour-long meeting over the stickiness of the new communion gloves with the lonely, curt cat-lady who's still pissed that we changed the words to the hymn "Good Christian Men, Rejoice" to be more gender-inclusive!?

Or as Jan Richardson observes as Jesus ran into forces other than God's in the temple in Mark, "Interesting, isn't it, that this encounter took place in a holy space? It's a great example of what I've seen time and again: that places meant for worship and seeking after God often attract the most chaotic folks. That which is opposed to God is often most drawn to those places devoted to God."[1]

It is for this reason, that during the trenches of ministry and the thick of infertility issues that the quote, "Ego sanctuario meo," became my first tattoo idea. Never had three words done a better job of encapsulating my long-winded essence, nature, goals, identity, longings, and values. Never have three words simultaneously comforted and catalyzed me.

Ego sanctuario meo. I am my own sanctuary.

Now, before you go running for the hills shouting, "Heresy, Heresy! She's discounting the institute of religion! She's discounting the faith community! She thinks she can do it all on her own

---

1   Richardson; *In the Sanctuary of Women*, 152.

like some independent, post-modern yuppie! She's taking the wheel back from Jesus! She's taking Christ out of Christmas!" hang with me here.

When I came across this quote, "I am my own sanctuary," it affirmed in me that the grit and peace that I cultivated did *not* rely on the choices of others. Adversity might momentarily redefine the process, but it doesn't completely derail the route to the goal. I call the shots on my emotional health and let others call their own. I teach others how to treat me, thus my source of affirmation comes from within. The correct psychological term for this is being 'differentiated' and was coined by Dr. Bowman. [2] In seminary we took *many* psychological exams to assure our level of differentiation was high enough to survive the gnashing of teeth that awaited us in the local church.

Ego sanctuario meo because as our youth directors casually threw around to keep us from pre-marital sex, "You are a temple of God, and God himself is present in you. No one will get by with vandalizing God's temple, you can be sure of that. God's temple is sacred—and you, remember, *are* the temple."[3]

The Holy Spirit dwells within *you* and the Holy Spirit dwells within *me*. And when I type the word "Spirit," I am referring to the "The *same* Spirit" Romans 8:11 teaches "that raised Jesus from the dead."

When I type the word "Spirit," I am implying that "deep within [you] is the wisdom of God, the creativity of God, and the longings of God."[4] Yes—*that* Spirit is within you. A shortage of grit and peace should never be a concern, for these are sourced

2   Nichols; *Family Therapy*, 78.

3   1 Corinthians 3:16-19

4   Newell; *Christ of the Celts*, 21.

from the Divine, cultivated by us and stored within our souls for whenever we need them.

Similar to what Reese With— I mean, Cheryl Strayed, felt as she hiked towards healing on the Pacific Coast Trail in *Wild*, "I was amazed that what I needed to survive could be carried on my back. And, most surprising of all, that I could carry it."[5] It took me a while to trust myself as my own fully equipped sanctuary. Not only did it take some time, but it took some work. I had to get intentionally acquainted with all the difference parts of *my* sanctuary.

From my body, to my mind (concepts, judgments, inferences); from my simplest emotion to the deepest yearning of my spirit (heart, will, character); *all* make up my soul, *all* make up my own sanctuary. And as Dallas Willard reiterates, *all* are interconnected and house the Holy Spirit.[6] Since some of the above terms have differing definitions, I will use Willard's definitions to categorize our journey together.

Our journey takes place in a season of transition, for I am leaving the church that I have served for nearly fifteen years as I write this.

While some of the information that I share with you will, in no way, be news, I hope that the fresh way that I have assembled this is enough to engage and encourage. I will simply share stories of discovering myself as my own sanctuary and my observations of said stories. I will also be doing some major name-dropping of folks who have assisted me on my search. If at any point during our chat you feel a need to set this down and *Amazon* one of

---

5   Strayed; *Wild: From Lost to Found on the Pacific Crest Trail.*

6   Willard; *Renovation*, 30.

their books, please feel free. This is your book, so open it, write in it and dog-ear-it however you see fit.

(Lame alert!)

As I printed out some of the first pages of this book, I literally hugged the stack and like a newborn, I asked of it, "What do you want to become? What stories will you grow to tell?"

Little did I know this second book that I birthed was already a teen and was *very* flaky with its identity and responded with, "I want to be a memoir on some pages, and then a self-help book on others, and sometimes I want to even read like a spiritual devotional of sorts. And I want to pierce my tongue like Jayna. Above all else, I think I was made to make the reader chuckle while she/he feels encouraged and equipped."

And like an earnest parent with the purest intent and the highest of hopes I said to the pubescent stack, "Go, be, do, my love, and tell the tales you were meant to tell."

So, on the following pages, you will read poems, lyrics, scriptures, blog posts, and an *insufferable* number of similes.

There are also many neurological studies shared. I am in *no* way an expert in this area, but I someday hope to be if the Mindfulness-Based Cognitive Therapist, Ruby Wax, would ever respond to me on *Twitter*. (Teach me your ways, Fair Ruby.)

The contents page, which is intentionally detailed so you can access any beloved section with ease, also reveals that the biggest chunk of the book is on relationships. This is, as you guessed it, on purpose. Since becoming my own sanctuary, I have been continually convinced that the love, grace and grit that we cultivate within are not meant to be hoarded but to be shared.

Each chapter also comes with reflection questions. (You are welcome.) Because as Edmund Burke shares, "Reading without reflecting is like eating without digesting." (And that's just uncomfortable for everyone.)

You will also notice that many comedians will join you on this adventure. Ever since I was a preadolescent human, I have been obsessed with the art of comedy. The ability to take another to the highest form of glee with one well-crafted sentence has always left me in awe.

One of my most beloved comedians of *all* time, Miranda Hart, addresses her readers as Dear Reader Chum. I would like to steal this from her; for although I have prayed for you, Dear Reader Friend, I have yet to learn your name. As I read Hart's books, I feel so cared for when I see, "Dear Reader Chum", and I desire nothing less than to make you, Dear Reader Friend, feel exactly the same.[7]

So, hence forth, ye shall be called, Dear Reader Friend, and it is my pleasure to serve thee.

With each chapter, may you welcome *all* the feelings.

If a paragraph cradles you, then rest in the nook of her elbow.

If a sentence strikes an uncomfortable chord with you, then seek the reason behind the offense. As Bob Goff said, "Know that what brings you to tears will lead you to grace and your pain is *never* wasted." God *is* faithful in healing.

If a parenthetical statement causes you to chuckle, then *literally* laugh out loud because chances are you need it and no one will care (except for that guy sitting behind you).

If some words dare you to act, then forge boldly ahead because let's face it—you *so* got this.

---

7   Hart: *Peggy and Me.*

With the reflection pages, may you gather your thoughts as you move with grit and grace. These lines are your confidant, your drawing board, your microphone, your stage.

By the close of the last chapter, may you know God a little deeper and trust yourself a little more. And may you be encouraged, for you *already* possess enough grace for every wound and enough grit for every goal within *sanctuarium tuum* (your own sanctuary).

CHAPTER 1

The Holy Within: The Differentiated Samaritan

I was once part of a Bible study group made up of a dozen or so women of all different Christian sects. (Side note: one must be extra-articulate with the 't' or else it sounds like something else—"secTs.") Most often the conversations were grace-filled and intelligent, but then there were other moments like this one:

A few of us were discussing the life-enhancing tool known as the *Enneagram of Personality*. Unlike other personality assessments, this one has spiritual roots and explores the relational systems of one's childhood as a cause for her current nature. It has helped many in keeping their egos in check and drawing them nearer to God. (Check out Helen Palmer, Dear Reader Friend.) As we discussed our "wings" and "false selves" with an unnecessary amount of passion, we were suddenly interrupted by, "I think personality assessments are sinful."

"Come again?" I laughed, assuming she was being funny.

"I think personality assessments are sinful. They take the focus away from God and put the focus on us and that's a sin," she proudly expounded.

I paused for a moment, attempting to control my extroverted tongue, and as a Three on the *Enneagram* with a strong Two wing, I replied as if these were the last words I would ever speak.

"I could see a smidge of truth in that statement, but what if there was someone whose days were the furthest thing from peaceful or joyful, and it was simply because her choices and surroundings were not honoring the way that she was wired? What if someone lacked all kinds of self-awareness and had no clue how to love herself well? Or care for her needs?"

Yes, all of that—I *literally* said all of that with great fervor; and looking back, I wish I would've added, "Furthermore, the Bible explicitly teaches of different types of gifting being giving to each of us. How effective are we if we remain unaware of these gifts?" (mic drop)

"Hmm, no," She said with a lazy shake of her head, unfazed by my etymological explosion. "God will guide us for our needs. Focusing on ourselves is sinful."

And just like that, the door of the conversation was closed.

REALLY?!

Is it though?

It is really sinful?

Really…?

Does it *really* hurt one's relationship with God to explore her inner terrain to assure she is revering how God put her together? Not to sound like Seth and Amy from *Saturday Night Live,* but…*really*?! This? *Really*? Honoring my limits and trusting my gifts is the same as me lusting after another man or murdering Hitler? *Really*? It's the same?

This?

Really!? A Sin?! *Really?!?*

What is it with us Church-folk?

If we're not flogging ourselves, we are equating the *Myers Briggs* with porn and shaming ourselves for liking our test scores. I'm pretty sure when Jesus said, "The first shall be last, and the last shall be first," in Matthew, He did *not* go on to say, "And those who hate themselves the *most*, and vow to never use their brain to become more self-aware shall receive honorable mention upon entering heaven." No…never happened. As Rick Warren teaches, Jesus simply desired for us "to think of ourselves *less*, not to think less *of ourselves.*"

And yet, we "holy-rollers" get it *all* wrong sometimes.

We deny our own self-care, in order to care for others and then walk around with our burnout like a badge.

I will never forget one Staff Parish Relationship Committee meeting I observed as a college intern. I had the "joy" of shadowing many pastors in the area, and this specific one was truly a cautionary tale.

The committee chair had asked for the Senior Pastor's report for this quarter and copies were passed around the table. My 19-year-old eyes were shocked by the bold words at the top. Ninety-six hours a week. Yep, his average workload exceeded the required full-time amount by 56 hours! Beneath that, a breakdown of how these were specifically spent with pastoral calls, sermon prep, committee meetings and so on. When the ill-equipped committee chair asked him if he thought this size of workload was wise, the pastor answered a seemingly different question with an aloof amount of pride, "My prayer life with the Lord will sustain me."

As I got to know this frazzled pastor, I discovered he was always like this. Sadly, the outlined report he had given me seemed to be the only thing about him that I could find impressive. He had no sense of self (his limits, his talents) and no routine of self-care.

He lacked the grit that derived from the fact that he and his calling were worth fighting for. And he lacked the deeply rooted peace that it would in fact be *God* pulling most of the weight in the fight. In his overly-committed life, he was never *still* enough to feel the peace of the Holy Spirit whispering, "You got this, because *I* got this. Now stop working 96 hours a week and take up napping as a hobby!" In the months to come, I sadly watched from afar as his marriage ended and a heart attack ensued.

Fear overtook me as a naive pre-ministerial student because around the same time that he reached burnout, another pastor-friend in town was let go by his congregation for asking for a sabbatical. Doubt filled my being. *Will this be me? Will the church eat me alive? Will I burnout before I am thirty!? Will I be incapable of authentic friendships, or nonetheless—normal human interactions? Was Nigel right in* The Devil Wears Prada *when he told Andy when her boyfriend broke up with her, "That's what happens when you start doing well at work. Let me know when your entire life goes up in smoke, then it's time for a promotion."?*

If some voices of my youth weren't confusing self-awareness with sin, they were surely confusing self-*love* with sin.

As I began serving at camps and presenting at conferences across the Bible Belt, Midwest and the East Coast, I came in contact with a cliché of Christian women that were much different than I. They preached a "homily of homely" if you will (trademark pending). It's as if their fear of sexually tempting their parishioners by looking "too feminine" (whatever the heck that means) made them vengefully turn into asexual beings that seemed to be genderless.

What do I mean by this? I mean they were *adamantly* against the pleasures found in the world of cosmetics and fashion.

Yes, these women, in the name of our great and glorious Savior, would show up to work looking like they just rolled out of bed. As a born and bred Southern Belle with the scarlet letter of a contoured face, I was quite struck at how they took *so* much pride in taking *no* pride at all in their appearance. As a Wanna-Be-Femi-Nazi, I admired their right to choose how they presented themselves. Thankfully, friendships grew despite a friend's belief that my vain lipstick was hurting my faith and my pierced ears were sinful.

Newsflash, Patrice, the apostle Paul was writing about specific women in a specific city in 1 Timothy who were worshiping a false god, not me and my eye-shadow! Gah, Patrice!!! [Insert eyeroll.] (Yes, that was meant to be read in the tone of the character "Robin" from the ABC show *How I Met Your Mother*.)

THE FANTASTIC

Both of these experiences point to a much larger systemic issue within popular Protestant theology that teaches you to fully deny your inward-most person. This disconnect not only robs us of the joy and beauty of exploring the inward person, but, as we learn from the Danish philosopher, Soren Kierkegaard, a relationship with God is distorted if it leads us away from a relationship with the self. Or, in Kierkegaard's own words, "The self is the conscious synthesis of infinitude and finitude that relates itself to itself, whose task is to become itself, which can only be done through the relationship with God…the self is healthy and free from despair only when, precisely by having despaired, it rests transparently in God." [1]

"*Whose task is to become itself…*" (And boom goes the dynamite!)

"And now that we are all twitching and drooling on the floor in the fetal position," as my late, *beloved* philosophy professor Chris Caldwell used to say, "let's unpack this in laymen terms."

Kierkegaard was wary that some had a perspective of God (the Infinite) which he termed, *the fantastic,* that would disconnect them completely from themselves— or the self/spirit."

"The fantastic is generally that which leads a person out into the infinite in such a way that it only leads him away from himself and thereby prevents him from coming back to himself." [2]

This not-so-fantastic-state (by modern use of the term), not only leaves one disconnected from self, but inadvertently connected to God in a warped way. It is for this reason that, "The greatest hazard of all, [is to lose] oneself…very quietly in the world, as if it were nothing at all." [3] Therefore, in order to know God deeper, one *must* know herself more deeply.

Whenever we emphasize or even *celebrate* the beauty of the self, we are in no way downplaying our relationship to God, but we are in fact commemorating God's stunning handiwork and the holy interconnectedness of all of God's creation. [4] It is for this reason that I am always blown away when intelligent,

---

1 Kierkegaard: *The Sickness unto Death*, 30.

2 Ibid., 31.

3 Ibid., 32.

4 Acts 17:28, Ephesians 4:6.

postmodern spiritual leaders feel guilty for taking time for self-care or disregard the value of self-love altogether.

PORCUPINE

I recall taking an emotional quotient test as a seminary student. This exam would "test" the health of our relationships with self (intrapersonal relationship) and with others (interpersonal relationships). I was stoked for this because my mom had always comforted me with the reminder that EQ mattered *way* more than IQ in the real world. But I think she might've just been lying to me whenever I was jealous of my two *very* academically successful sisters.

Regardless, I knew my EQ, unlike my IQ, was sure to impress and, for the ultimate confidence boost, it did. Sadly, I could not say the same for most of my friends. While the hope was that our class would all score around seventy-percent out of one-hundred, many sadly scored in the forties. We servant leaders suck at being nice to ourselves sometimes, well—most of the time (apparently).

How do we improve upon this? How do we learn to love ourselves enough to *rely* on ourselves? How do we let the confidence of our inner and outer beauty enhance all other areas of our lives? How do we not get sucked dry by the needs of others while also being in healthy personal and professional relationships? How do we let others do their own emotional work without bringing us down in the dumps with them? How many questions is enough to get this point across? Five? Seventeen?

We succeed at these things by learning to juggle our human needs of individuality and needs of togetherness.

Or as psychologist, Dr. Murray Bowman calls it (and the goal that my counselor and I are working towards), we aim to become "differentiated beings." As such, one does "not respond automatically to emotional pressures [of others] and has the capacity to reflect and act wisely in the face of anxiety."[5] This is one reason why the imagery of being one's own sanctuary spoke to me. Regardless of the poor choices, overreactions of others or general stress of my surroundings, I am safe and can think strategically within my own skin.

"Where an undifferentiated person finds it challenging to maintain their own autonomy, especially around anxious situations, a differentiated person has the ability to resist the pull of emotionality"[6] from others. As a differentiated person, even as a Christian, I have come to realize that I am only responsible for my *own* emotions, and I let others be responsible for theirs. And at the end of the day, this is all I really have control over in my life—not the weather, not my child's behavior during family photos, and not who wins *The Voice*.

An enlightening visual, as shared by psychologist, Deborah Luepnitz, for what healthy differentiation looks likes is porcupines in the winter. (Hang with me. I have a point. *Punny!*)

When porcupines are cold and wish to stay warm, they must cuddle for warmth to survive. However, if they cuddle too closely, they will harm each other with their needles. So, the goal is to find the healthy proximity for warmth without pokes. The goal is to maintain her pokey individuality without sacrificing their piney togetherness. [7]

---

5   Nichols; *Family Therapy*, 78.

6   Ibid, 78.

7   Gilbert; *Committed*, 223-224.

Before years of counseling and some intentional discomfort at seminary, I was a *highly* (H-I-G-H-L-Y) undifferentiated person. As Bowen teaches, the relational habits of my upbringing followed me into my professional relationships. Like the "fortunate fool" on a stage that Jack Johnson sings about, I *performed* daily with hopes of impressing everyone and *my* mood was at the disposal of another's reactions. This is not a good thing when you live your life in a fish bowl as a nineteen-year-old church intern.

With church being extremely personal to many, some have eccentrically *strong* views about how things should be done and how a church employee should act (dress, date, and dance). I had *no* life outside of the church, and when I look back, I honestly don't recall that much from those years. I was constantly frazzled and my mind was operating out of survival mode, i.e. I was rarely ever mentally present.

This state of emotional (un)health did not set me up for success during tense interactions.

I recall falling apart when I was asked by a church matriarch to go home and change before attending a church reception because my $100 Liz Claiborne khaki outfit was not formal enough. I abided.

I regret not standing up for myself one Saturday when I was chewed up one side and down the other for returning the communion dishes two-hours late. I had worked *beyond* overtime that week to host a women's retreat, and they weren't even going to be used until the next day anyway.

My first (and hopefully only) nervous breakdown occurred when several holy-roller friends of mine literally "unliked" me when I protested their idea to protest worship services due to a lesbian serving on the tech team. If I did not impress others or if another disagreed with me, the day was a complete failure—I was a complete failure. (Geesh! Talk about a real whack-job!)

As I graduated and entered the "real world," the unhealthy ways of being undifferentiated continued.

My husband's shirt morphed into a tissue after many stressful days of serving in the church. I would cry on his shoulder as parents were annoyed with me for giving Bibles out to kids who were not church members (true story). Tears would flow whenever I was bulldozed by well-intended senior coworkers, or whenever triangulations would take place. At the slightest sign of tension at a meeting, I would shut down emotionally out of fear that I might offend someone with my alternative views.

These situations are not unique to me, of that I am certain. Multiple talented, young people with a surplus of empathy and a low self-esteem are taken advantage of in other ministerial positions as well. It's as if, as Kelly Ripa said when Strahan did what he did (he *knows* what he did), our "politeness is viewed as passivity," and our range of talents exclude us from basic human needs.

Congregations often forget that ministers are *people* first and foremost.

We are people capable of feeling *all* emotions.

We are people who desire and require an identity outside of the church.

We are people who have the right to occasionally disagree with you (in a loving, well-rehearsed, diplomatic way).

And finally, we are each just another person. Not a person that is both fully divine and fully human. We are each just another person like you.

What I am getting at is that although some ministers might have a Messiah complex, *none* of us are Jesus. None of us were

32

birthed from the holy womb of Mary. Emmanuel, none of us are. We should not be worshiped for our preaching styles, beliefs or personalities. We should not receive all of the credit for the church's successes (as limply defined as that may be), nor all the blame for the church's areas of growth. We are *just* people following a divine nudge to serve other people in the name of the Lord.

Fortunately, my seminary experience equipped me as a differentiated person, and I was finally able to honor my preferences and trust myself in the midst of disagreements. Whether it was me harmonizing by ear while I led in the praise band, the Christmas tree in the Fellowship Hall being moved, or the placement of the prayer in the service, my favorite phrase to use with overly-reactive parishioners was, "I really do not appreciate the tone you are taking with me."

This was often followed with me shakily saying, "I know this is not your preference, but I ask that you trust that I am doing what is best for the church and we can review the result together after-the-fact as we plan for next time."

Yeah, my husband witnessed one of these reactive moments once with a parishioner and said I sounded like a conflict-resolution textbook—word-for-word. By that time, I probably had one or two of those books memorized.

Instead of shutting down emotionally during intense meetings and replaying SNL sketches in my mind (true story), to lower my blood pressure, I would take deep breaths and do a mindfulness exercise (more to come on this) known as a grounding exercise. Once I was able to slow my heart-rate down, I would simply start asking questions about said sticky situation. These tactics made it easier for me to remain a non-anxious presence. Don't get me wrong, I still replay SNL sketches in my mind during meetings, but it's only during times when we are debating the color of carpet in the foyer or the outreach ministry of stray cats in the alley.

As a differentiated person, I did not lose my super-power of empathy. I could still feel what people were feeling, but I was able to do this from a distance (in a sense). I was able to be moved by their emotions with boundaries, and with this, as Brené Brown teaches, came *increased* compassion for them. While I was the one being empathetic, he/she was still the one in charge of his/her own emotional health—not me.

Becoming a more differentiated person was not only a benefit for my personal life and my sustainability in ministry, but, frankly, it improved the health of our entire team. As Bowan teaches, any change in behavior by one member of the relational system will have some effect on the relational system as a whole. Like in a game of chess, " my opponent moves in relation to my moves. One change on my part changes my opponent's strategy too. By holding myself accountable for my own emotions and reactions, I implicitly held others accountable for their own (at least in their interactions with me). By teaching others how to treat me as Dr. Phil says, some ended up treating themselves and others in a healthier way as well. I was also a better teammate because I could think clearly about decisions and authentically do what was best for the ministry as opposed to doing what I thought others would find agreeable or impressive.

CHARTRES

I truly was growing into *my own* sanctuary, like the legend of the mighty French church, the Chartres Cathedral; regardless of the surrounding stress, I had discovered that the sacred and secure strength *within* was sufficient to sustain me. (You are welcome for that *scrumtrulescent* alliteration.)

The year was 2001, and I was a wee lil' high school freshman raising my head to take in her glorious stained-glass windows. There was a herd of us young Methodists standing outside. My sister and I joked about the hunchback and Esmeralda (like naive Americans who thought it looked just like the Notre Dame cathedral). However, this holy fortress told a very different story.

For over fifteen-hundred years, the Chartres site has been a space of Christian worship. While it had withstood may fires during the Dark Ages, one finally took it down in the 11th century. The locals gathered together with plans to not only rebuild but to upgrade it. And that they did. Through emotional, financial, and physical support, the townspeople erected a superb structure that, to this day, baffles historians and architects. No records remain that detail the cost to create one of the grandest churches in the world.

The Crusades took place during her rebuilding, but since the locals believed that war went against the way of Christ, the men were sent to help build the Chartres Cathedral instead. In 1200 CE the final touches were made. The famous labyrinth, with its six-petaled rose in the center that represents the Lord's Prayer was set in the middle of her nave.

While it was flooded with tourists, it still felt holy for me to step in its path. The tour guide shared that the cathedral once housed a school and the labyrinth, a crucial part of their curriculum. I recall thinking about the *millions* of souls who had prayerfully strolled before me. I recall thinking of how, although we lived at different times, my spiritual journey was somehow in step with theirs.

I could go on and on about the beauty of the labyrinth, but there's more to her mysterious legend to share. Over the centuries, not only was she a stunning and sacred cathedral that was built out of peace and love, she was also *unexplainably* strong.

Throughout the French Revolution, other churches were robbed and obliterated. But the Chartres Cathedral stood untouched. Kathleen McGowan shares, "Although the violent and destructive revolutionaries got as far as the foot of the cathedral steps, they turned back before entering the church and simply walked away from it. Through two world wars, when bombings had destroyed other Gothic structures across France in places like Reims and Vezelay, Chartres was again spared any damage. Chartres was built with a very specific intention toward peace, with a foundation of faith and service, and it holds that intention to this day within its stones. It is God's place, built by God's children, and protected by God." [8]

Now while the mysteries of this true tale might be a little much for some straight-laced-skeptics, I think all could get on board with the idea of living as *your own* Chartres cathedral; for you are.

You *are* your own sanctuary.

You *are* a house for the divine.

You *are* unexplainably strong.

You *are* full of peace.

You *are* untouchable to the outside chaos. (You really are.)

HOTEL BILL

So, what does living as your own Chartres Cathedral look like?

---

8   McGowan; *The Source of Miracles,* 98-100.

What does serving others while preserving your autonomy look like? How can you compassionately lead with firm boundaries?

To find the answer, we turn now to a snarky discussion between Jesus and a lawyer.

The lawyer tried to test Jesus with a question on earning eternal life. As Jesus often did, his concise answer led to an action step on the listener's behalf. He pointed the man in the direction of the law, that read, "You shall love the Lord your God with all your heart, and with all your soul, and with all your strength, and with all your mind; and your neighbor *as yourself.*"[9]

These final two words, "as yourself" are often missed as permission or a *mandate* to love ourselves well. Jeanne Stevenson-Moessner points out that it is easy for us to "miss the interconnectedness of these three loves: love of God, love of neighbor, and love of self."[10] While it is nearly effortless to love the first and easy to fake love for the second (#SayinItLikeItIs), the third is easier said than done; especially when one feels overcommitted, overly-tired, and undervalued.

After the law is shared, Jesus in a sense says, "Game on, Lawyer!" He then shares the parable of the good Samaritan. Now while it is awesome how Jesus puts this lawyer in his place by suggesting an unclean Samaritan would be a better neighbor than the overly religious, this scripture also has much to teach us on serving others as a differentiated person. It has much to say about self-love. As you read Luke 10:29-34, be looking for any help the Samaritan had and how his own plans changed.

---

9   Luke 10:27, NRSV.

10   Stevenson-Moessner; *A Primer in Pastoral Care*, 47.

"But wanting to justify himself, he asked Jesus, 'And who is my neighbor?' Jesus replied, 'A man was going down from Jerusalem to Jericho, and fell into the hands of robbers, who stripped him, beat him, and went away, leaving him half dead. Now by chance a priest was going down that road; and when he saw him, he passed by on the other side. So likewise a Levite, when he came to the place and saw him, passed by on the other side. But a Samaritan while traveling came near him; and when he saw him, he was moved with pity. He went to him and bandaged his wounds, having poured oil and wine on them. Then he put him on his own animal, brought him to an inn, and took care of him. The next day he took out two denarii, gave them to the innkeeper, and said, 'Take care of him; and when I come back, I will repay you whatever more you spend.'"

Did you catch it?

The Samaritan displayed self-love as a differentiated person by "managing to care for the man by delegating some of the responsibilities (to the innkeeper)," not altering his original plans in lieu of the man's personal issues, "and then following up with aftercare." And in so doing, he maintained his autonomy in a potentially sticky relational system and "he avoided compassion fatigue."[11] With these choices, the Samaritan took steps towards a more sustainable future. This parable illustrates such a lovely balance of being self-aware enough to care for ourselves *and* others. Or as Bowen would say, it teaches a healthy balance of togetherness and autonomy.

The interesting thing about this balance of which Bowen speaks is that it is a paradox to live it out well, for the rise of loneliness in the U.S. is on the rise because we are too often forgetting about ourselves.

---

11   Ibid, 47.

As Dr. Emma Seppala teaches, "The answer to loneliness may be to pay attention to the person who is not paying attention to us—the person who stopped caring for us: our own self. We [are] so lonely because we don't take care of ourselves—whether lack of time, energy, or interest, or simply because we don't deem ourselves important enough. Sometimes we feel so lonely because it is *our own friendship* we are longing for. [...] It is an act of love for yourself to [physically, emotionally or spiritually] nourish yourself."[12]

Unlike the frazzled pastor I mentioned before who had completely forgotten about his needs and goals, this Samaritan, in some way, exemplifies successfully living in this paradox. What would it have looked like if that pastor would have followed the Samaritan's differentiated example?

He could have set a firm boundary with his staff/parish/relations committee that he would strive to honor a forty-hour work week (except on the rare occasion when there are four weddings and a funeral). The tasks on his plate that were not in line with his talents could have been delegated. These two changes *alone* would have freed up Friday nights for dates with his wife. What if he had viewed himself as his own Chartres Cathedral, responsible only for his own emotional health regardless of the surrounding emotional chaos? He would have felt more comfortable saying, "no," and would not have relied on the emotionally-fickle parishioners for affirmation.

If he would have trusted himself as his own sanctuary, his necessary grit and grace from within would have prevented his burn-out. He would have cultivated grit for the days when others didn't like his decisions and grace for days when he didn't like

---

12   Seppala; *The Loneliness Paradoxes*, 100-101.

his decisions. And this cultivation would not have been his own doing, for within his own sanctuary resided the Holy Spirit. As J. Phillip Newell shares, "Deep within [you] is the wisdom of God, the creativity of God, and the longings of God."[13]

NAMASTE

The divine moves and breathes within the neurons of our brain and the marrow of our bones; and as I tell my daughter, "The divine is always speaking to us, but the voice will sometimes sound differently than other voices; so, if we still our brains and quiet our bones, we will hear from the One who made us, who knows us, and loves us."

Have you forgotten that you have such an arsenal of Holy?

If you have, in a few pages, may you be reminded that you do. And if we revisit the scripture from a few paragraphs back, we find much more depth awaits us in the metaphor of being one's own sanctuary or temple, if you will.

1 Corinthians 3:16-19 reads, "Do you not know that you are God's temple and that God's Spirit dwells in you? If anyone destroys God's temple, God will destroy that person. For God's temple is holy, and you are that temple."

While it's easy to read this as an anti-bikini verse (as many have), this is not (at all) what the early church leader who wrote it had in mind. Paul believed that each member of society had the option to tap into the Holy Spirit which resided within, and those that did collectively made up the Church—God's true temple.

See?

---

13   Newell; *Christ of the Celts: The Healing of Creation*, 21.

It's never been about dress code; your body is a temple as it houses the Holy Spirit. Paul cautioned that in our communities, our *togetherness,* we must be wary of dissension and division for this will destroy the temple of God in a double-sense. [14]

And it is *only* in owning our identity as a sanctuary that houses the "wisdom, the creativity and the longings of God,"[15] that we can live out our togetherness as a vital part of the community. Within this community, we all have been wired with different talents (1 Corinthians 12:8-10), and it is *only* in serving one another *with* said talents that the fullness of God is experienced (1 John 4:12).

As a chubby teen who took Yoga to get ripped, I was introduced to the term "Namaste." While this once Hindu, now secular, term is not explicitly Christian, I think it holds much theological value. In saying this with a bowed head at the end of each class we are inherently saying, "The divine in me bows to the divine you." My sanctuary which holds the divine honors your sanctuary which equally houses the divine.

How beautiful, yeah?

This conviction changed my self-esteem, and I took this new perspective with me while I traveled with my missionary grandparents. Once at an orphanage they were building in Matamoros, Mexico, my grandfather *quickly* learned that I lacked the skills to join him in building cinderblock walls. As a prideful teen, I stuck with it, but after many mistakes, he "encouraged" me to return to a task that was in line with my talents. Luckily, painting the fingernails of the orphans was a reasonable alternative.

---

14   Barclay; *The Daily Bible Series: The Letter to the Corinthians,* 34.

15   Newell; *Christ of the Celts: The Healing of Creation,* 21.

"¿Puedo pintar tus uñas?" was the first complete sentence that I butchered in Spanish. This was such a sacred time of sparkly pinks, and the aroma of acetone. I would paint one of the girl's nails and then she would turn and paint another's, and before too long a domino-effect of recognizing the divine in another through service occurred all throughout the orphanage. Like many who travel and serve in similar ways, I was surprised at how the Holy Spirit was so active within their lives. I was surprised that they ministered to me *more* than I to them. #cockyAmerican

It is only in recognizing yourself as a differentiated sanctuary that houses the Holy Spirit that you can fully recognize this in others. From your body, to your mind; from your emotions to your spirit, the divine is moving through every part of your person. But let's follow our ole' youth director's example in his poor exegetical work with 1 Corinthians, and let's put *way* too much emphasis on the physical body.

I am my own sanctuary.

*My being houses the Holy Grit
and grace come from within,
regardless of the choices of others.*

AS YOU FORGE ONWARD AS YOUR OWN SANCTUARY, ASK YOURSELF:

1. What is the relationship between a warped view of self and a warped view of God? When was a time that your skewed view of self hindered how close you felt to God?

2. How would a current stressful situation feel different if you assumed the posture of your "Chartres Cathedral" whose emotional health was protected from the outside chaos and you let others be responsible for their own emotional health?

3. As one in whom the Divine dwells, you already possess the necessary grace for every wound and grit for every goal. If you could mend a relationship based on this, would you and which one? Or if you could chase a goal based on this, would you and which one?

CHAPTER 2

Grace for My Body: A Temple Tuned-In

STRIPPER

I once dated a stripper.

I did not know he was a stripper at the time that I agreed to the date, but he was a stripper and I did in fact date him. I should have known he was a stripper at first glance, what with the product-filled hair, insane body (not to objectify you, Sir Stripper), and fake-bronze glow. But these clues were less obvious in his *PF Chang's* uniform.

While my two sisters, mom, and I dined, a blonde waiter with Drew Carey glasses approached us with waters. After taking our order with an excessive amount of banter, my mom suggested that I ask for his number because "I should date someone like that."

Yes, the man who we had known for three minutes was apparently my soul-mate. (Thanks, Mom.)

As usual, I kindly thanked her for the "suggestion" and politely changed the subject. It was an exciting time for my sisters, and there was much to talk about on their visit. The younger one, beyond academically and athletically impressive, was starting her junior year at high school. The older one was coming into her own as a young educator. As we joked, shared, and dreamed, we quickly became a table of laughing hyenas.

We inhaled our lettuce wraps, and Mr. Tight Pants kept returning to refill full drinks. He was quickly sucked into our ridiculousness. We learned that he was studying computer science and this was one of his *two* jobs to support his studies. The sapiosexual within me was highly impressed with how articulate he was.

After about an hour-or-so it was time to check out. He brought us the ticket and on top of it was a fortune cookie that had been cut in half, but placed back together. He handed it to me and walked back to the kitchen. Sealed inside the wafer-of-an-envelope was a little slip of paper with his number on it. I freaked, and my mom and sisters began urging me to go talk to him.

Now to say that I was socially awkward in flirting situations would be the understatement of the century. As one who came out of the womb a workaholic, I would approach guys as if we were making a business deal. I would not be the first one to speak. I would be emotionless (so, the opposite of a flirt), I would stick to the facts and wrap it up with a confident handshake; just like Jack Donaghy taught me.

And this is exactly what happened in *PF Chang's* that day.

Gathering my gumption, I slid across the sticky, unnecessarily large booth and went to find him. He was already serving another table, so I waited by the kitchen entrance, because that is what normal people do? He spotted me as he was refilling another's coffee, grinned, and headed toward me. My nerves got the best of me. I began talking really fast, "Hey, I just wanted to let you know that I got your number and that I would be very interested in making these arrangements. Thank you so much for this offer and when is the best time to contact you?"

Nailed it. I had this flirting thing down!

He laughed (I mean—who wouldn't after that uncomfortable display), and said, "Cool. Yeah, just whenever. I'd love to hang."

"Yeah, great." I stammered, "Let's hang. So…. I guess I'll call you and you won't recognize my number, but it will be me calling." Looking back, maybe I didn't want to go on a date with a hot metrosexual based on the nonsensical words I was saying.

He laughed again and said, "Yeah, I know, I will answer."

His eyes were darting around the room at his tables, so I knew it was time for me to wrap up this "meeting" with a firm handshake and the ole' post-worship pat on the top of the hand that was being shaken. And that was exactly what I did.

Flirt well? Check!

He smiled confusingly, and we both said our goodbyes.

I called him that night and the following weekend we were on a date. As I contoured to Mariah Carey's "Fantasy" (the ultimate get-hot-for-a-hot-date-song), my mom called to give me the usual advice of, "How about try actually flirting? And maybe don't talk so much?" I was only half listening to her though. On this night, my excitement was louder than her critiques.

As it was the first date, we reasonably drove ourselves to a very nice restaurant. While the conversation was adequate, I found myself unreservedly distracted. It was *very* apparent that he spent a *tremendous* amount of time on his body. Pants and shirts had never fit that way on the praise band members that

I usually dated—on any man I had ever seen, to be frank. *Who was this guy?*

We chewed and chatted and very early on he shared that he was stoked for his new work playlist.

"That's nice that they let you listen to music at *PF Chang's.*" I said.

"Oh, no, not there. For my other job." He replied dabbing his chiseled chin with a napkin.

"Oh yeah—what's that?" I said as my mouth searched for my straw.

"I'm a stripper." He nonchalantly replied, "Is that weird?"

I nearly spit out my water and before I could speak, he said, "Sorry, I should have told you before. I just wasn't sure how you would have responded. It is a weird gig, but it pays *so* well, and it really helps with school and—"

My laughter interrupted him, "You've got to be kidding me? Do you know what my job is?"

"Are you a stripper too?" He said with a sly smile.

"Nah, I'm too short." (That was my lame attempt at a joke.) "I serve at a church as one of the ministers." I said with a chuckle.

"No way!" He said, "Well, check us out! A minister and a stripper? We're just like Jesus and Mary Magdalene."

And Dear Reader Friend, it was at that exact moment that I should have followed my mom's advice, but I just couldn't let one of the apostles *to the* apostles be misrepresented. Not on my watch! And surprisingly, after my *long-winded* spiel on how *The* Magdalene had been mislabeled by the Catholic church as a prostitute for centuries, and that there are sacred, non-canonical texts telling more of her story, he was still up for going to see a show with me.

The traveling acrobatic show was nice, but for some reason, he was not that interesting to listen to when he was not sitting in front of me. (I'm shameless, I know.) I quickly realized that the only thing we had in common was that we were both fans of his body. By intermission, I had decided that there would not be a second date.

On the way back to my car, he took my hand and held it as we walked and talked. This surprised me, and I thought, *Oy vey, you're not going to like what I have to tell you.* When we got to my car, he chivalrously opened the door, and right as I was opening my mouth to break the news to him, my words were stopped by his lips.

He pulled me in at the waist for a deeper—albeit subpar— kiss. *Every* inch of him was touching me. His pecks felt like two burly shields. As my fingers caressed his back, I felt more muscles than I knew existed. I had never been embraced by such physical strength before. It felt as though I was making out with a veiny bicep. While I knew our lifestyles did not match and he was the *furthest* thing from "marriage material," the inner-voices of standards hushed and I just kissed back.

Now, we'll get back to this frothy moment later ("Frothy" is my mom's ladylike term for "#$*&@."), but for now I want to pause and talk more about his body. (Because we haven't done enough of that already, right? *Dude. Was. Ripped.*)

Underneath the sheer attraction to his physique was my *utter* jealousy towards him. During this season I would preach in sports bras as to hide my womanly curves (that I had detested since I was a tween), and here he was prancing around with great pride for his body. There was a part of me that envied him, a part of me that wanted to *own* it and rock it like he did. Yes, both of our bodies were temples, but unlike me he was *quite* proud of his. I wanted to be proud of mine too, and flaunt it with satisfaction; in a modest way, of course, like the occasional fitted shirt or a two-piece.

But, alas, I could not be so lucky to share his view. Having no life outside of the church had left me completely afraid of my vagina and ashamed of my D-cupped figure. Ever since the fifth grade, I can recall sucking it in in front of the mirror, just wishing that I was a less substantial being. I am sure I am not alone in these thoughts, for the struggle (and the body-shaming) has been real since (and well-before) biblical times.

BREAST MILK-DRINKING NUNS

Instead of a "temple" the Greeks sneeringly labeled the body as a temporary "tomb" which would someday pass away. This school of thought was known as Gnosticism, which argued the body and all matter were pure evil.[1] What mattered most was solely the spirit. The spirit would not overtake us with desires of sleep, food, and sex. Unlike the spirit, the body would be escaped from at the end. It was for this reason in Corinth that they did *whatever* they liked to and with their "tombs," and quickly rose to being one of the most immortal cities in the Bible.

This, of course, led to much debate when the apostle Paul rode into town, preaching on the body as a temple (not a tomb to which we are shackled) as we read in 1 Corinthians 6:19. Paul believed that while, "the stomach and food are passing things; the day will come when they will both pass away. But the body, the personality, the [person] as a whole will not pass away; [he/

---

1   Winner; *Real Sex,* 34.

she] is made for union with Christ in this world and still closer union hereafter."[2]

It is during the works of Paul and other New Testament authors that the Greek word, *porneia,* appears fifty-five times. Isn't it interesting that the issue of human sexuality comes up more in the New Testament than the word 'orphan' (forty-times) and (a word similar to) 'hell' (less than ten) in the *entire* Bible?

As you can tell from the root of this word, *porneia* deals with illicit sexual behavior and some verses could translate into pre-marital sex. These scriptures on human sexuality, though, have often been read through what the ivory tower scholars call, "proof texting" which is where readers pick verses out of context and string them together to support an argument.

In exploring the cultural context of some of these passages however, one sees that a woman's virginity was imperative in the business deal of her dad and husband when she was "sold" into wedlock. Some believe that these verses stem more from this point than the point of God's mandated abstinence. In fact, many go as far as hypothesizing that marriage was an altogether different beast in the middle east two-thousand years ago than it is in the US in [Insert year that you are reading this.]. But these are only educated guesses.

Regardless of *porneia's* explicit meaning, it is clear that as the early church grew, its leaders spent much time on the fact that since God gave us such a sacred and supernaturally powerful gift as sex, it *must* come with some major responsibility.[3] But since the body was perceived as that from which to escape, many did

2   Barclay; *The Daily Bible Study Series: The Letter to the Galatians and Ephesians,* 56.

3   Winner; *Real Sex,* 39.

not attend to these teachings and treated their bodies (and entire beings) poorly through sexually unhealthy behavior.

Paul would need back up in correcting this misinterpretation, and it would take the ancestors of our faith quite a while to come around to the truth. (Thanks, Gnostics!) However, one major perk arose from this lie regarding our bodies during the twelfth century through matriarchs like Christina the Astonishing.

She was a self-harming, mental health advocate, and nun, whose body was of very little value to her (hence, the self-harming). Like others, her sole focus was on the pious ways of her thoughts and feelings. In fact, she believed that her sweet breast-milk was God's reward for her piety, so she would drink it as sustenance. And while some might have doubted her sanity, it was during her life that the, "focus on the soul enabled women to release themselves from the physical inferiorities ascribed to their gender in order to achieve the status of an authoritative figure."

These medieval female leaders would derive strength from their souls as opposed to what was viewed by others as their lesser than bodies. While this perk bared major fruit in their ministries, there was still some major body-shaming going on. Christina was sadly ahead of her time with regard to the flogging trend and would angrily beat her own breast and body and shout, "O miserable and wretched body! What is to you that you keep my wretched soul in you for so long? Woe to me, who am united to you (body)."[4]

Fortunately, her successors brought forth a much healthier, holistic perspective and appreciation for the body. One matriarch of our faith in the fourteenth century, Catherine of Siena, emphatically taught of the intertwined nature of the body and

4   Cantimpre, 449.

the soul and how, "the soul could improve the physical state of the body." [5] A century later, another saint Teresa of Avila, complimented her perspective with proclaiming how "peace of the body would restore peace of the soul."[6]

SPIDER WEB

These matriarchs of the faith were on to something that neuroscience would confirm years later, and that is how our emotional sensations affect our physical being and vice versa. Or as Dr. Ash Ranpura puts it, "The brain and the body are connected like a spider web made out of many neurons. When an insect gets trapped anywhere in the spider's web every single string on the web vibrates. The spider can feel that vibration from any point on the web. The brain and the body are like that, they're totally interconnected, a single system. Anything that affects one part affects the whole system."[7] Studies even suggest that one's mood (with the exception of those who struggle with chronic depression) could manually be altered by "opening up [one's] chest, lifting your head and going for a walk."[8]

Crazy, yeah?

To further unpack the lovely, interconnected way we're all designed, the Buddhist monk, Gelong Thubten states that, "Our body never lies. Our mind can play all kinds of avoidance tricks on us, but the body will *always* tell us how we feel. It's important

---

5   Hanson; Connections Between Body and Soul, 30.

6   Blog, Dan Burke, *Peace of Body, Peace of Mind from Teresa of Avila*.

7   Wax; *How to be Human*, 68.

8   Ibid, 70.

to listen to that. Sickness, for example, is a messenger—it can be a wake-up call to get us to see what's going on in our minds." [9]

It is important to listen to our bodies. As part of our sanctuaries, they are trustworthy navigators through our lives.

As a very anxious child, I carried all of the world's problems in my stomach which led to an ulcer at the age of ten. As I shared in the intro, certain environmental factors were not exactly setting me up for success, emotionally. Eventually, the fear and worry led to an insane pain in my upper stomach, a very bland diet, and a decade-long relationship with Prilosec. (We're talkin' such pain it would take me to the floor in the fetal position instantly. No bueno.) This is not surprising since as Dr. Ash Ranpura says, "the stomach processes so much information long before it reaches our brain and we cognitively put words to it." [10]

As the stomach is the second brain with, "its vast neural network", too much anxiety being held here for too long can negatively affect ones physical health over time. Thus, the endless cycle of emotionally feeling like shit to physically feeling like shit begins. This will make you think twice next time you're tempted to not trust your gut won't it? [11]

By the time that I graduated college, I had learned to manage my stress-level with more play, stillness, and healthy friendships. Not only was my constant tummy ache gone (along the prescriptions), but I was able to focus on the things that mattered most in life like drinking coffee and eating chocolate.

---

9   Ibid, 70.

10   Ash Rapura, *Ruby Wax in conversation with a Neuroscientist, a Monk & Louise Chunn*. Penguin UK, Interview.

11   Brown, *Hackspirit.com*.

About a decade later, a family member of mine made a horrendously vile choice, and while I thought I was worried sick, a new bodily sensation had made itself known within me.

To impress you with medical jargon, the ulcer scar on my mucosal lining was not shouting at me like it had when trauma would arise. I felt nothing in my stomach, actually, *but* I felt tension in my forehead.

What was this feeling?

This sensation? It was hot and unabashedly moved through me like a soldier on the front lines. A feeling with such force I had never felt before. It was truly enlightening to me that I noticed and labeled it physically before I intellectually named it.

I was *angry*, not afraid.

My younger self was fearful—no, incapable of feeling this. Good little Christian girls don't get angry, right? But as an adult I was angry to my core and pissed off with every cell in my being.

I. Was. Mad.

As lame as it may sound, I thanked my body for helping me "name it to tame it" as Dr. Tina Payne Bryson says. My body was leading me on a clear path towards healing—healing for myself and healing within my family. If I had not been tuned in to *and* trusting in my body, I would have confused this emotion as something different and would have reacted *much* differently.

Conducting oneself out of fear looks *much* differently than conducting oneself out of anger. Anger, unlike fear, is not hesitant or passive. Anger, towards injustice, births a higher voltage of courage. Acting out of anger is like—well, we're not at that chapter yet, so let's return to our bodies.

Our bodies are the furthest thing from temporary "tombs." They are our sages, our guides, and *imperative* parts of our own sanctuaries. Your body was "fearfully and wonderfully made" [12] by the divinely creative Creator.

Your body was made to dance and to hug, to sense and to act, to move swiftly and rest sweetly. Your body was made to get goose bumps when Lauryn Hill sings *His Eye is on the Sparrow* (*YouTube* it!) and to erupt with laughter when Kristen Wiig plays *Sheena* on SNL. (*YouTube* that too!) Your body was made to experience beauty and to do "good works."[13]

Our bodies were made so that you and I could be the hands and feet of *Christ*. It is quite sad that the church has been so anti-body for so long (and many still are), or simply quiet about the subject matter. And often when it is spoken on, confusing (and sometimes harmful) messages are shared.

PURITY RING

The confusing messages that shaped me were probably from the church conforming *too* much to its culture. Being raised in the Bible Belt, every day was a dichotomous pageant in which I needed to look good enough for men to want to sleep with me, but I was forbidden to think about/desire to/or sleep with a man. (Even the *notion!*)

This was truly a perplexing standard, but I tried—and I tried hard. In my pubescent mind, I saw it as an easy opportunity to receive the acceptance and affirmation that was absent in my house at times. All I have to do to be good *enough* is keep my pants on like a good lil' Puritan!? Sign me up, society! When can I be measured for my chastity belt?

---

12   Psalm 139

13   Ephesians 2:10

Now how often is it appropriate to tell others about my purity ring?

Twice a day?! Only on Sunday?!

Or then is that a sin too because I'm bragging?

Oh well, I will just tell others if they ask.

And so, I did.

During my first month of high school theater class, we were asked to share two goals as an icebreaker. (Yep—everyone was still getting acquainted with each other.) When it was my turn I confidentially shared with this mixed-age group of students that I wanted to be on Broadway and not have sex before marriage. I thought I was *so* cool, but as the cookie usually crumbles, I was the *exact* opposite. The room erupted with laughter and the curt theatre teacher (as they often are) laughed and said, "Wow, that's a lot of information that I don't think anyone cares to know. Next person, please!"

But why didn't they care to know about it???

Is that not a measurement of my moral character? Isn't that how I proved I am close to God—a real Christian? Isn't that how I am better than all of the other girls who actually have boyfriends to go too far with? This is a competition of chaste, and I want to—I will win it. Just give me an A+ for a low libido or a medal of asexuality, Ms. Theatre Teacher, because my sense of worth depends on how you think of me right now, and I want you to think I am a good girl who keeps it in my pants.

Yes, obviously, I was a *highly* undifferentiated teenager. I would always feel so sorry for a fellow teen who would cry at a church lock-in out of shame for going all the way with her boyfriend, before gloating about it to my grandmother and mother to assure they knew that I was not like her.

I had withstood the temptations of the flesh! (Pat me on the back someone!) Since I had no life outside of the church, even my weekends were spent at holy-roller retreats, and while spiritual disciplines, sacramental worship and acts of service came up, the majority of the curricula was focused on keeping our V-cards.

Dear Reader Friend, some of these church-retreats were *so* intense on sexual purity that you would have thought that the second century Christian thinker Tertullian, who taught that original sin was encapsulated and passed through a man's semen, was in charge.[14] Yep, we are talkin' *intense.* And as Lauren Winner points out in her book, *Real Sex,* that would have saved me a lot of grief in my teens, these retreats were filled with lies such as: premarital sex will lead to eternal damnation and a horrible sense of self, men need/want sex more than women, and that our bodies are gross and unimportant. (Screw you, Gnosticism!)

I remember thinking that if their curricula had spent more time building us up in our talents, we would naturally make better choices in our dating because of an increase in one's confidence. One has little time for rebound make out sessions if she's too busy as a student council officer or the lead in a play. I also had to chuckle a bit when we would spend an entire day on sexual purity at an all-girl retreat, only to be surprised by our teen-male waiters at a banquet that night. I was so confused.

Are not my hormonal feelings bad? Yet, you invited all these guys to be all dressed-up and chivalrous to me? What am I supposed to do with this? Is what I'm feeling the Holy or the horny moving through me? Is this a test?! Is that why there is an empty seat at the head of the table for Jesus, so he can see clearly to grade my interaction with

14   Shroyer; *Original Blessing,* 154.

all of the hotness in this room? Give me a big fat 'A' for abstinent, Sweet baby Jesus!

I AM SO CONFUSED, CHURCH!

It's like that time Disney used the Jonas Brothers' sexuality to *market* purity rings and uphold their "pure" image. What the what?! How does that even make sense, Mickey?![15] (Remember? Even Kenny fell for it.)

I guess it makes sense for the church to harp on this since less than three percent of Americans are not having sex outside of marriage,[16] so many take advantage of the gift of sex. *Still,* doesn't God care more about my pure heart than my pure hymen? I used to think this when I finally discovered what a hymen was (and that I had one) when I was twenty—I mean, a teen.

The neurotic guilt I struggled with as a teen after hot-and-heavy make-out sessions was enough to make me tap into my inner Christina the Astonishing and shout, "O miserable and wretched body! What is to you that you keep my wretched soul in you for so long? Woe to me, who am united to you (body)." I was *so* hard on myself. I would tearfully jot down prayers of forgiveness in my journal.

Why did I touch his leg? My mom said never to touch a boy's leg, and I did it anyway. Stupid, stupid Meg! Why did I keep on kissing him? Just keep it in your pants so that Jesus will love you, and you will finally be good enough! If you go too far, the church board

---

15   This is a reference to *South Park* episode 1, season 13. Kenny and his new girlfriend are encouraged by the Jonas brothers to wear purity rings, which is secretly a marketing tactic by Disney to sell sex to their young viewers.

16   The Guttmacher Institute. "Trends in Premarital Sex in the United States, 1954-2003." *US National Library of Medicine*, Public Health Rep. (2007 Jan-Feb) :73-8. https://www.ncbi.nlm.nih.gov/pubmed/17236611.

will find out and you can't sing in the choir anymore because only the celibate can sing in the church choir. God help me next time to honor my "boundaries in dating" (My favorite book in high school. Yep, cool...I was *so* cool.).

While the feeling of making out felt *so* good, I hated my curves for making me like *my* potential sexiness. (And this followed me well into my twenties.) As was illustrated on a date with my then fiancé, where we were gathering eggs (#Kansas) and he was explaining to me how the chicken's eggs were their menstrual cycle. And my dumbfounded face and juvenile questions about female anatomy forced him to point to my lower abdomen and jokingly, yet seriously ask, "Do you know how *all* of this works?"

No. No, I did not. I was oblivious and terrified of my vagina.

What's that down there?

No clue and I'm not gonna be the one to find out because that would be sinful!

Around this time, I met a gal who was the Lucia to my Punchinello.[17] Like the wooden people in Lucado's book who gave each other dot stickers for their flaws and golden stars for their accomplishments, I felt weighed down by the stickers from the church and society regarding my body and my purity. Then, in walked Hilary.

She was an honor student and a cheerleader who was the epitome of kind and (get this) a Christian. She walked with a confidence of which I could *only* dream; and behind her, left a trail of dots from the church on her purity and stars from society on her independence. Being the epitome of differentiated, she

---

17 A reference to Max Lucado's *I Am Special.*

was not out to impress anyone, so their opinions would never stick.

I idolized her, though I'd never admit it.

One day by our lockers, Hilary was sharing that her mom had talked with her about different forms of birth control and encouraged her to talk with her when she was ready to make certain choices with *her* body.

Correction! Thought I, the High School Pharisee. *That's not your body, Hilary, it's the church's and they have* a lot *to say about what you do with your (whisper this next sinful word) 'vagina.'. Do you want me to call your mom and explain that to her? I'd be more than happy to. It's really important that she be clued in on this.*

I was greatly befuddled by Hilary's self-esteem. She talked about "her" body and "her" choices with great honor. She was not giggling out of teenage hormones but was communicating with maturity about a serious subject—a sacred milestone.

In the years to follow, Hilary would share in private of the first time her boyfriend (now husband), like the unwed lovers in the Song of Solomon, climbed her sturdy branches and drank *abundantly* from her sweet milk. There was no shame in her voice, only joy. She felt cared for and respected. She chose the day and (apparently) called a lot of the shots during the act. And because of the honest talks with her mom years in advance, she was prepared with birth control as well. To my surprise, the guy didn't even paint a red letter on her chest and dump her after his original-sin-filled semen entered her.

Amazing.

While Hilary *truly* inspired me, I was not emotionally mature enough then to actually learn from her strong sense-of-self and quickly reverted to my old, unhealthy ways of slut-shaming her to my mom and grandma. I am in *no* way proud of this, and continually seek forgiveness for the *many* female friends that I have slut-shammed over the years (through gossip sessions that we holy-rollers reframe as "Joys and Concerns"). Throughout my high school years, I developed more and more into Mandy Moore's character from the (fantastic) satirical film, *Saved.*

Out of a lack of love for my own body, I was extremely condemning of others and absurdly terrified that others would find me flawed or impure.

I thought my platform of purity was a common worldview held by my peers.

Didn't every teen fear being kicked out of the church choir for making-out the night before?

No. They did not. I was mistaken.

As an upperclassman, I had been dating a guy for a month. Like any hip chick does, I was talking about my purity ring in his Bronco in my driveway.[18] He then shared the *devastating* news that he was *not* a virgin. My heart dropped. I had really liked this guy, and now I would have to (obviously) break up with him because as they said in youth group, "You can't put a used toothbrush back in the package," and there was no way I was letting him put his used toothbrush in me. I tried to hide the shock on my face, kept the convo short and went inside.

My mom greeted me from a dark kitchen, as she doused the kitchen with bleach for the fourth time that hour. (We were a strange upper-middle-class family who *rarely* turned on lights to save money. So. Strange.) I told her the sad news that I would be breaking up with him because he was not a virgin like me, and

---

18   Let it be known, Dear Reader Friend, that I did not break up with him that night and he brought much joy to my, until then, *very* dull high school experience. We are still good friends, and he is someone that I respect and admire.

"once you lose your V-card, Mom," I said hoping to make her proud of me, "you can't get it back."

[Insert pageant-like-wave of the purity ring.]

She confusingly stared at me, which I took as an invite to share more (a mistake most extroverts make).

"Everyone knows that since he has been intimate with someone already, he *can't* be intimate with me. Our relationship was basically over before it started because he's not a virgin like me." I preached.

She sat the sponge down as her face went from confused to *utterly* disappointment. She then poured on the guilt like gravy on biscuits. "Meg, how can you just judge him like that!? Who are *you* to judge him like that?! Sometimes things happen and people make mistakes, but it's OK. You can't just break up with someone because of a difference in opinion."

I stood silently for a moment, mainly because I couldn't breathe due to the bleach, but then a bewildered sadness came over me.

Why aren't you proud of me? One's V-card is everything, Mom, everything!!! I did the right thing. I am just holding him to the same standard that our family and the church have shoved down my throat. Why is it much easier to overlook his error of judgment, than it would be for mine? Why the double standard, Mom, why? Does God seriously not care if he gets some tail, but I can't? Why can he go all the way, and I'm told not even to touch his leg? Why is no one giving me a gold ribbon for doing the right thing?!

HAPPY MEAL

Hearing an opinion that differed than the church's continued to catch me off-guard as I matured(?) into my twenties. During some of my summers as an undergrad student, I served as a chaplain at a sailing camp in Long Island. My boss and friend, Greg, encouraged me to explore seminaries nearby, so we ventured over to Union Theological Seminary. I had romanticized this visit so much in my mind because such theological greats like Bonhoeffer and Niebuhr had served there.

My heart leapt for joy as we walked down the lovely grey stone hallways. The energy in the space was electric until we opened the door to the admissions counselor's office.

The guy's nook was an utter disaster with stray paper and fast-food bags all over the place. He was a substantial man with his feet propped on the desk and his stained shirt partially untucked like a Texas high school football coach. *Bonhoeffer would be appalled, sir! Tuck your shirt in! Sit up straight and, for God's sake, throw your McDonald's bag away!*

It turned out he not only looked like a lazy Texas football coach, but he also addressed me like a player which made this exchange quite comical. We explored some of their master's programs, and as the conversation moved towards housing options, he said something most unexpected. "Yeah, you can live with, sleep with whomever you like. We know we all have different views here at Union, and we encourage diversity."

Come again? Am I in the right place? Did you just encourage promiscuity? Are you implying that I should not take the sacredness of my body and what I do with it seriously? Did you not notice this giant cross purity ring on my hand, sir? [Insert pageant style wave of the ring.] *Also—how can that stain be from BBQ sauce? It is ten in the morning. Have you not changed since yesterday?!*

On the drive home to Camp Quinipet, I thought of how while I did *not* appreciate the fear-based teachings of my childhood on sex, I *most surely* did not appreciate the lackadaisi-cal, happy-meal-smelling tales of promiscuity of that guy either.

So, what was a happy medium? Could I learn to love my body and my libido? What is a libido? Is it even real? If a libido increases in the woods, and no one is around to hear it, does God care? Could I live from a healthy view of myself and my sexuality that would not allow the pendulum to swing too far in *either* direction? If so, what would this look like?

I would grapple with these questions for *eons* and the memo-ries of the Bronco, the bleach and the BBQ stain would pop back up while I was on a second date with the stripper years later, as he said to me in his muscular glory, "So a minister huh? I gotta ask ya one question that I've never understood. What's the deal with Christians and sex? Why do y'all hate it *so* much?"

Well, you extremely hot man, let me tell you.

A lot of the credit for this fear of and distaste for sexuality goes back to the fourth century. It was at this time that instead of being a religion, Christianity morphed into an empire. With this immense shift, J. Philip Newell teaches that, "our natural sexual attractions and longing for physical union being regarded as among the deepest and holiest expressions of the dance of the universe," were skewed as "opposed to the rhythm of God's being" and "a tragic separation was introduced between the spir-itual and the physical."[19] This worldview also affected our doc-trinal beliefs, and even though the early New Testament manu-scripts make it clear that Jesus had siblings and the prophetic words used in Isaiah 7:14 is "young woman" and not "virgin," Mary's permanent virginity began to be revered. In no time at

---

19   Newell; *Christ of the Celts*, 55.

all, chastity was held as a superior spiritual path than tying the knot.

Newell goes on to expand our minds to the fact that in John's gospel, Mary is never referred to as a virgin. He writes, "she is a mother. And in no other gospel is she more honored, but it is because she is a mother, the conceiver and bearer of sacred life, not because she" eternally had her V-card.[20] While we will get to know Mary a bit more later, it is hilariously worth noting that by the fifth century, the church's view of sex had become so distorted that they believed that the holy semen must have entered through Mary's ear because the Holy would have had nothing to do with one's naughty bits. Ridiculous.

"If [these views] had not done so much damage," Newell proclaims, "we could just describe them as deluded. But they represent the tragic severing of the spiritual from the physical and the holy from the sexual that has worked untold havoc in the hearts and lives of countless men and women through the centuries and continues to do so today. Of course, our sexual energies are infected with selfish desire and have been linked to some of the most horrific acts of domination and abuse in the history of humanity, but it is precisely because we have forgotten the holy root of sexuality that we continue to forget how it is to be truly expressed."[21]

While my view of sex and my body were just as shaken-up and skewed as Mary being impregnated through the ear, my grit to maintain my V-card was *unshakable*. And unlike the holy-roller gals I hung with that "kissed dating goodbye" (another book that will *not* help you in the flirting department), this was

---

20   Ibid., 56.

21   Ibid. 57.

a little more difficult for me because I was *actually* dating. And for your amusement now, Dear Reader Friend, I will list the nicknames that my family and friends gave the men of my late teens and twenties:

- "The-Devil-Made-Me-Watch-Porn" Guy: I was out of this one about ten seconds after hearing that.

- The "Looming Friendship Guy": The lesson here, Dear Reader Friend, is that if someone is not willing to call you "Girlfriend" after a *year* (Shame on me, I know.) of committed frothiness and describes your relationship (?) as a "looming friendship", you recede from him as *quickly* as possible.

- Spoiled Prince: This one broke up with me for being "too Methodist." (Yep, he was a non-denom guy who was not so hot for a high-church gal.) When I wouldn't end it with Wesley, he ended it with me.

- Socially-off Youth Minister: Dude was *uber* awkward, as is sadly the case for many church staffers. #RealTalk

- The Stripper: Really doesn't need a nickname, does it? Dude was a stripper!

- And my all-time favorite...Stoner-Jesus: Self-explanatory really, dude looked like Jesus, if Jesus smoked a whole a lotta pot.

While I have no regrets (not even one letter) of how I was romantically physical, the relationships above were *filled* with shame, self-abasement and a horrible body image. As far as my story is concerned, I do *not* regret waiting. However, I highly regret my *motive* for waiting. I regret the *terror* that I felt about my body in these relationships. And like a shout in a cave, this shame of being sexual (and being a sexual being) reverberated within me until three weeks before my wedding night.

I had done it. I had played by all of the rules. I had earned grace. I was twenty-four and I hadn't let any guy drink the milk for free. I was a virgin. I'm not sure what more of a turn-on to me was: how impressed my church members would be to marry off a grade-A virgin, or the idea of sleeping with my husband. (If I'm being honest, it was probably the first one, because I was clueless as to how totally awesome sex was.) Everyone would be so proud of me. I beat the odds. So few were as strong-willed as me, and guys enjoyed the chase of 'neurotic-guilt-girl'. I had to most certainly be an abstaining role-model for all.

I pretentiously spoke loudly at the doctor weeks before my wedding when I was getting on the pill. I loved the look on her face when she asked a second time to make sure, "And you've never had sex—like, ever?" Maybe another nurse would hear and be impressed by what little fun I had been having.

"Nope. I'm saving myself for marriage." I said, as my hot air filled the room.

One young nurse did hear and she called down the hall through her laughter, "Gina, come here. This woman's a virgin."

I sat up proudly on the foot of the examination bed.

Gina quickly ran down the hall as if I was a bearded woman at a circus.

She said, "What?! You are? But why?"

I cleared my throat and cockily said, "I'm just a very religious person, a minister actually, and this is what we (I) do."

And as they both looked back at me, I realized that they weren't impressed by or proud of me. They didn't envy me or even understand me. They seemed to have pity for me.

I didn't think too much of this moment, because I was kind of a dick, and didn't think that the opinions of the unchurched mattered. I also only shared that I was a virgin to one up them and to make myself feel better about myself. Mission accomplished. (I also realize now how unprofessional this whole moment was as I relive it nine-years later.)

However, in the weeks coming up to the *most* important night of my life (as I was brainwashed to believe), these nosey nurses triggered within me great doubt.

I had spent my whole preteen, teen, and young adult years making choices *solely* based on impressing the church, and for what? So I could sit here like some arrogant ass in an examination room and make two fellow women feel less than? This doesn't even make sense. This isn't even a fun result—a worthwhile prize. Most importantly, this is the *furthest* thing from godly behavior. Were all the times I slid out of the back-seat of a car leaving many a male with blue balls worth *this*? Shouldn't sex be more explosively beautiful than this perfunctory chore, this obligatory show-pig I had made it into? (In the Midwest, we have fairs where livestock are shown in a pageant-like compet— you get the point.)

Was this what I had been waiting for?

What had I been waiting for?

If I hated being abstinent, and the only reason I was waiting to share my milk was because that I *honestly* believed that the church had controlled every aspect of my life (including my vagina), then this was not the start to my marriage that I had dreamt of when we drew our future husbands back at those ole' purity lock-ins.

I wanted to take my life back from the church, and for me there was one way to do that.

My husband wanted me, just me, not me as the mouthpiece of the church. My husband and I neither one wanted the cloud of witnesses with us in our honeymoon bed beaming over us with tearful pride as we awkwardly read lubricant labels.

So, three weeks before my wedding night, I took back control.

I took back the control of my values.

I took back the control of my thoughts.

I took back the control of my feelings.

I took back the control of my desires.

I did all of this by taking back the control of my body from the church.

And I did this by laying with my fiancé in the biblical sense.

No one was allowed to have any say in this decision. For the first time, it was *all* me—and him (obviously). I, Meg, was in charge of what my body was capable of and. It. Was. Perfect.

This decision, which set the standard for my sex life, was the most shameless, spiritual decision I've ever made. I felt, for the first time, a *complete* love for my body *and* for my sexuality. I felt that God loved me, Garrett loved me, and that my neurotic guilt around pleasure was doing *nothing* but hindering my quality of life.

That night taught me that the body is *not* something to escape nor is my sexual body something to vilify.[22] And above all else, It's OK (even fun) for me to be sexy. I have also learned over the years that the tempting fun of promiscuity that I once found enticing cannot compare to the sex between a committed couple. As Laura Winner explains,

"The sex of blind dates and fraternity parties even of relatively long-standing dating relationships, has, simply, no normal

---

22   Winner; *Real Sex,* 94.

qualities. Based principally on mutual desire, it dispenses with the ordinary rhythms of marital sex, trading them for a seemingly thrilling but ultimately false story. This may be the [most twisted lesson of premarital sex]: that [casual] sex is exciting. That sex derives its thrill from the instability and drama. In fact, the opposite is true: the dramas of married sex are smaller and more intimate, and indeed it is the stability of marriage that allows sex to be what it is." [23]

[We must allow sex to be ordinary.] This does not mean that sex will not be meaningful. Its meaning, instead will partake in the variety of meanings that ordinary life offers. Sex needs to be clumsy. It should at times feel awkward. It should be an act we engage in for comfort. It should also be allowed to hold any number of anxieties –the sorts of anxieties; for instance, we might feel about our child's progress in school, or our ability to provide sustenance for our family. Sex becomes another way for to people to realistically engage the strengths and foibles of each other. Not only sexual intercourse is transformed as we allow it to take on the varieties of the commonplace; the varieties of the commonplace themselves are transformed as well.[24]

(And Yes, I know that Winner would be perturbed with me quoting her directly after I shared my tale of premarital sex. Lo siento.)

In retrospect, it was the way that the Union guy downplayed such a sacred and powerful gift that irked me so. I, of course, couldn't have articulated this then because I wasn't gettin' any.

But now that I experience the empowering, uniting, and comforting nature of sex, I'm even further confused as to why Mr. BBQ stain lowered the bar for his students. Why would he *not* want his students to aim for the best? Why settle for second-rate, fast-food-smelling, greasy-fried, synthetic-filled-snack-like

---

23   Winner; *Real Sex*, 119.

24   Ibid, 81.

hook-up? Why not aim for what sex could be—what it was *meant* to be—the replenishing, satisfying, scrumtrulescent feast of lovemaking?

I look forward to discussing such quandaries with my daughter someday when she's old enough to know that a tampon is not actually a giant q-tip like I told her it was when she pulled one out of my purse at Target. #shes3

DEAR DAUGHTER

Dear Henley,

This is bound to be an uncomfortable conversation. It would be for anyone. I think this is because so much of our world misunderstands sex. So many don't know what to do with this gift. Regardless of the discomfort that your questions and my answers might bring, please know that I am here to affirm and educate you.

No matter what you hear at school or on [Insert future form of *Spotify*], sex *is* sacred and supernatural and sometimes I wonder why God gave us (often) stupid humans a gift with *such* power, for with this power comes *great* responsibility. [Insert #hornyspiderman if hash tags are still a thing.]

As the pastor and writer, Frederick Buechner, teaches, "Contrary to Mrs. Grundy, sex is not sin. Contrary to Hugh Hefner, it's not salvation either. Like nitroglycerin, it can be used either to blow up bridges or heal hearts."[25] (Of course, there will be footnotes in the letter to my daughter. Who do you take me for?)

---

25   McCleneghan: *Good Christian Sex*, 9.

Your dad and I trust that you will handle this gift with great responsibility, and we would encourage you to share your personal boundaries with those whom you *choose* to be romantically physical.

When it comes to creating your boundaries, don't ask questions like, *Will this make me less holy?* or *Will I be less loveable by my future spouse?* Instead, try (actual helpful) questions like the ones in Margaret Farley's book, *Just Love: A Framework for Christian Ethics.* These would be such questions as, "Will this physical act show respect toward myself and my partner as persons or am I using him/her as a means to the end of pleasure? Am I respecting my own autonomy? Or is this physical act what is best for our relationship at this time?"

I would love to read this book with you and discuss it as she unpacks these criteria for love in a highly applicable way. Tools like these will equip you to move with intentionality as you grow and mature.

If I would have had Farley by my side as a young person, I would have carried around less shame. However, I have no regrets about my dating life as a teen and adult. I had *a lot* of fun with guys before your dad, and those moments were filled with mutual care and respect. While I think there is something special about your dad being the only man with whom I have slept, I am fully aware that your story might read differently. And my personal story in *no* way diminishes the sacredness of another's journey of sexual exploration. (Yep—I heard it, that was awkward. Won't say that again.)

Above all else, I want you to know that I'm here for you, because this (although it's sacred and supernatural) is *just* another topic that you and I can talk about (as long as you feel comfortable with the conversation).

Because as my spiritual director, Danielle Shroyer teaches, "[We should, when we view our lives as one of original blessing from God, and *not* through the lens of our own sinfulness] approach sex with far more perspective and sanity. Sexuality is not bad, but it isn't everything either. It is one part of the human experience, and is to be given its healthy and rightful place. In a broader sense, original blessing carries far greater opportunity to respect and value our bodies, rather than contribute to a culture of shame…and negative body image. If we are taught to see our bodies as the source of our sin nature, it's not particularly easy to appreciate them, much less to know what to do with them. When we believe that *our bodies are good*, we can choose to live into them as a natural part of human life *blessed* by God."[26]

As you soar through middle school and high school, may you pour your heart into your friendships, homework, and hobbies. May you have a blast discovering your talents and dreams. Know that at the right time, romantic love and the opportunity to *be* romantically loving will present itself. There's *no* need to seek it out. And no matter what the church tells you, your feelings are *not* sinful. Your body *is* beautiful. Being sexy (at the appropriate age) *is* fun. And lastly, you *do* have a hymen and a libido; they don't just appear (and then disappear) once you put on a wedding ring.

I love you *more* than life itself,
Mom

I am my own sanctuary.

---

26   Shroyer; *Original Blessing,* 156.

*My being houses the Holy. Grit
and grace come from within,
regardless of the choices of others.*

*My body is beautiful;
a gift that should be cared for,
trusted, and never feared.*

AS YOU FORGE ONWARD AS YOUR OWN SANCTUARY, ASK YOURSELF:

1. What is a lie that you heard growing up about your body that you would like to correct? Correct it with the *truth* now in ink.

2. When was a time that while, "your mind played all kinds of avoidance tricks on you, your body did not lie to you and told you exactly how you felt" about a situation? Did you listen to your body then? If not, why not? If so, how did that work out for you?

3. Why *did* God give us (often) stupid humans such a powerful and sacred gift as sex? How does it harm one's sex life to *not* view it as a supernatural gift?

CHAPTER 3

Grit of My Mind: A Water-Walking Mentality

"Let our connections get you places and your reputation keep you there," my campus minister, Rev. Ashlee Alley Crawford, used to say as we were all finding our place in the world. This was definitely the case for the first major conference I landed as a speaker (a goal that had been on my heart since I was a teen).

BIG GIG

To this day I *still* don't know how I got in, except for a professional connection that I had. A niche-mate (what recovering workaholics call "very accomplished persons") of mine, Matt Guevara, was the Executive Director of the International Network of Children's Ministry who encouraged me to apply for their Orlando conference.

Now it is not me typing humbly when I express my shock that I had actually gotten in. Allow me to set the scene. There were over four hundred choices of presentations and roughly one hundred would be selected. Conference attendance would surpass two thousand, and I was a complete and utter nobody. Sure, I had my first book coming out soon, but the names I competed with were on the covers of multiple books.

As I applied, my equally-sensitive, yet much-more-realistic husband, Garrett, monitored my inflated hope. The chances of my talks being selected were very slim—nay, non-existent. However, we both looked at this as a way of getting my foot in the door, and for the mere opportunity to apply, we were thankful. We also appreciated the idea of leaving the frigid Midwest in January for sunny Florida. So, we resolved to (try to) be grateful with whatever the results were.

After three weeks from the date we were informed we would hear back, I was (obviously) bummed by the silence. Rejection is a hard pill to swallow and this season taught me the lesson from Jon Acuff of, "Never judge your beginning on someone else's middle!" I needed this lesson as I was comparing my humble start to the glamorous middles of such greats as Adolf Brown, Tina Payne Bryson, and Ruby Wax. While I might have similar goals as these amazing communicators, I have lots of growing to do before my days will resemble theirs and that is OK.

As per how life goes, it was after I had come to terms with the rejection that the acceptance letter came. Garrett and I reread it *multiple* times out of disbelief and I even called the INCM Big Dogs to assure that they had meant to send it to me. Somehow, I had been selected to present not one, but *two* times, along with serving on a panel in a third session. What the What?! Three times?! I was just getting my foot in the door and now my feet are in three doors?! Seriously? What? Me?! I?! Yes, I, the unknown rook with a lot of grit and a lofty goal was somehow selected.

After sharing the joyous news with my staff, my ole boss who is the real-life version of Michael Scott from *The Office* gave me a pep talk, "Don't you think for one second that you don't belong at that conference. You are no longer a rookie. You have earned this spot and you have *a lot* to teach others. So be open, be humble and go to learn from others, *but* at the same time, walk with a little more swag. You belong there."

Because he is the real-life Michael Scott, the term 'swag' was an acceptable word for a sixty-five-year-old to use.

His playlist of support sounded far better than what was playing on repeat in my head.

Holy crap. How did this happen? I can't compete with these other speakers. I don't even know how to download YouTube videos yet for my presentation. I'm not off-script yet; I only have one book out. This is my first big conference; I don't serve in a megachurch. I'm a mainline Protestant; My setup crew is my mom and my grandma. The crowd will hear me and instantly regret their decision. (Let it be known, my negative self-talk *never* plays the age or gender card, and I have my family to thank for that.)

But then, empowered by the Holy Spirit, I adopted my boss's words about me as my own, and I began to believe them. This should not have surprised me since the brain uses the same area for talking to others as it does for one's inner monologue, and by simply imagining these words to be true, "a physical and biological occurrence [happened within] my brain and body" and every part of my being *lived into* these words.[1]

I did belong here.

I was *made for this*.

God *can* use me to equip and encourage others.

---

1   Wax; How to be Human, 26.

I have prepared very well, and I have *great* passion for these topics.

Most importantly--this was going to be a blast!

I got up early to pray and meditate each day before I spoke, and within my cells, the Holy Spirit would shake the message through me.

You think I would bring you here without a message worth sharing? You got this, because I got this! Now get up there and do. Your. Thing. Do exactly what I made you to do.

And, as many other times in my life, my favorite verses, Psalm 139:1-14 (which just happened to be the theme of this conference, #omen), comforted me. And because it's my favorite, I am going to share the whole kit-and-caboodle with you.

> "O Lord, you have searched me and known me.
> You know when I sit down and when I rise up;
>   you discern my thoughts from far away.
> You search out my path and my lying down,
>   and are acquainted with all my ways.
> Even before a word is on my tongue,
>   O Lord, you know it completely.
> You hem me in, behind and before,
>   and lay your hand upon me.
> Such knowledge is too wonderful for me;
>   it is so high that I cannot attain it.
>
> Where can I go from your spirit?
>   Or where can I flee from your presence?
> If I ascend to heaven, you are there;
>   if I make my bed in Sheol, you are there.
> If I take the wings of the morning
>   and settle at the farthest limits of the sea,
> even there your hand shall lead me,
>   and your right hand shall hold me fast.
> If I say, "Surely the darkness shall cover me,
>   and the light around me become night,"

even the darkness is not dark to you;
the night is as bright as the day,
for darkness is as light to you.

For it was you who formed my inward parts;
you knit me together in my mother's womb.
I praise you, for I am fearfully and wonderfully made."

I was made for this.

HDMI

Thank goodness that I had set myself up for success with positive self-talk because everything was far from rainbows and unicorns. Some things *did* go wrong. As a lover of lists, I will now share with you, Dear Reader Friend, a list of how the it-shay hit the an-fay during my debut as a conference presenter.

- The convention center's Wi-Fi was down. This was no bueno since I had a Prezi and non-downloaded YouTube clips. (As another, actual professional presenter pointed out to me, "You didn't download your clips? It's super-easy." *Yeah—maybe for you, Mr. Hot –Shot! Turns out he was right; it is super-easy.*)

- My RGB to HDMI adapter that I got for only $7, performed like a $7 adapter and froze all of my keys on the computer.

- I had many more attend my sessions than expected, and I didn't have enough handouts which in my mind are the meat of a session because they hold the personal application part.

- The company I was working with to sell my book totally forgot about our arrangement, and, since they were not my publishers, some of the reps were not too keen on my mingling with potential buyers in their booth in the resource center, as they weren't making any profits from my sales. #HatersGonnaHate

But my Holy-Spirit-Inspired self-talk sustained me.

I quickly found out that I knew much more than their Tech/AV team, and this was a much-needed confidence boost to me in the thirty minutes before I went on. I downloaded my Prezis into Adobe files (due to the lack of Wi-Fi), and then simply laughed at myself for making the mistake of not downloading my clips before-hand since (as every intelligent person knows) once the Prezi was morphed into this format, the clips would not play. While I was heart-broken, because the clips were pivotal pieces, this mistake of mine turned out to be a blessing in disguise. If the video clips had played, my sessions would have run late. Without them, I was able to present without feeling rushed.

As the ole adage goes, "The more prepared you are, the more spontaneous you can be." This was exactly what I was.

I used a white board to record their thoughts after small group discussions in place of the clips; and the clips that I just couldn't present without, I described in great, (unintentional) tear-filled detail. The finale of the movie *The Best Christmas Pageant Ever* perfectly summarizes our hopes when we create moments of worship for children (the basis of one talk), and as I shared this scene and pictured little pack of Herdmans experiencing the palpable, healing presence of the Holy Spirit, I just started (subtly) ugly-crying.

This unplanned cathartic moment was used by God to calm my nerves, quiet the sounds of my ego, and looking back I think it also humanized me a bit, which is really what everyone wants from a presenter.

When the other publishing company forgot about our arrangement and in no way offered me the marketing help that I was earlier promised, I shifted my goal for the day. I redefined success. *OK, I can do this. I can adapt. Today's goal is simply to mingle with folks and see if any of them would be interested in equipping their team with* The Bluebonnet Child *(my first book) book club.*

Yes, I was a rookie at speaking at conferences this size, and, yes, there were plenty of much more qualified speakers there. However, I *too* was called to be there, gave it my best, and loved EVERY flipping second of it! Even though things went wrong, my overall evaluation score was high enough that I was (some-how) asked along with eight other speakers to preside over select-ing the speakers for the following year. (What? How?) Most importantly, because my self-talk was helpful and I remained open to what I could learn, my first big speaking gig taught me so much about this beloved goal mine.

- Download *YouTube* clips. (Duh!)

- If I wanted to perform like a professional speaker, I needed to be willing to spend like a professional. So, I dished out $25 for my next RGB/HDMI adapter.

- Use Google slides just in case there is no flippin' Wi-Fi in a massive convention center.

- As one who always plans much more content than is needed for workshops, this opportunity taught me that I needed to allow much more time for the personal appli-cation part for folks. While we got out on time in the sessions, our time for processing and application was cut short. I still regret this for the participants.

- I was reminded *more than ever* of the power of being nice to myself. I learned to give myself grace for using index cards because: I was a mom of a toddler, working 40 hours a week at a church and college, and liked being with my husband instead of memorizing. So even though one person wrote on her evaluation that she wished I would have memorized my presentation, I can read her evaluation and think, "Yeah, me too. And that will come in time, but for right now, in *this* season of life, giving my best to God and to you, takes the form of index cards that I have rewritten and shortened five plus times." (But, don't be fooled the second time I was invited back to speak, I was totally off-script, baby!)

PIANO

This formative moment was *beyond* anxiety-ridden; however, because I placed my mind in a content, confident, and calm space, I was able to rise to the occasion, serve people well, and polish up my gifts. In Orlando, how I talked to myself was key.

As Victor Copan shares, "Our beliefs have the power to change us. Optimistic thoughts and positive thought-patterns have the power to heal our mind, our body, and our relationships. Conversely when our thoughts and thought patterns are based on negative or damaging ideas of information, this has the power to destroy us psychologically, spiritually, and physically... [Our] thought-processes actually change our brain structure. In other words, your thoughts, beliefs, and expectations can heal you—but they can also kill you."[2]

Our holistic health is not only affected by how we talk to ourselves but it's also affected by what we imagine. Neuroscience teaches that there was not only power in me being nice to myself as I prepped for Orlando, but (even cooler) by me visualizing myself as a successful presenter, my brain began operating as if I *actually* was one.

There was once a study done by Dr. Pascual-Leone of the National Institute of Neurological Disorders and Stroke, in which two groups of pianists were compared. The first group physically practiced the piano, and the other group just imagined rehearsing. None of the participants had ever played before, and all were taught the proper positions, and heard the notes correctly before the experiment began.

The persons in the "mental practice" group were asked to sit in front of a piano for two hours a day, five days a week and *think* about playing the notes while they heard the correct notes played. The "physical practice" bunch actually played the assigned sequence for two hours a day, five days a week. All participants had their brains mapped before, during, and after each day's practice. At the very end of the experiment all persons were asked to play the series of notes while a computer measured their accuracy.

The findings were incredible. Pascual-Leone revealed that both groups achieved the goal of mastering the piece and all showed similar brain maps. Norman Doidge reflected on the findings, "Remarkably, mental practice alone produced the same physical changes in the motor system as actually playing the

---

2   Copan; *Changing Your mind,*92.

piece. By the end of the fifth day, the changes in motor signals to the muscles were the same in both groups, and the imagining players were as accurate as the actual players were on the third day. The level of improvement at five days in the mental practice group, however substantial, was not as great as the actual players were on the third day."[3]

Whether one is trying to improve as a pianist, speaker, or [insert your future title here], by simply imagining oneself *as* this, the arrangement of neurons and nerve cells are rearranged, as if we *are*, physically, emotionally, spiritually and mentally *this* aspired title. Whether we are doing it or just wishfully thinking about doing it, many of the same parts of the brain are activated. And this holds true for every dimension of our life—for every type of goal. The Little Engine That Could was right after all. By visualizing success, one's performance automatically improves.

CONTRARY WINDS

One of Jesus's closest friends Peter often failed to visualize the intended goal and instead, was just highly reactive—towards himself and others. While he might have been instinctually acting from a place of love, he was nonetheless. And his way of functioning is the most apparent in Matthew 14:22-33.

> Immediately Jesus made the disciples get into the boat and go on ahead of him to the other side, while he dismissed the crowd. After he had dismissed them, he went up on a mountainside by himself to pray. Later that night, he was there alone, and the boat was already a considerable distance from land, buffeted by the waves because the wind was against it.

---

3   Ibid, 103-104.

Shortly before dawn Jesus went out to them, walking on the lake. When the disciples saw him walking on the lake, they were terrified. "It's a ghost," they said, and cried out in fear.

But Jesus immediately said to them: "Take courage! It is I. Don't be afraid."

Here was Jesus, after a draining day of ministry, just needing a little breather. Their insane earthly expectations for him were too much, so here he is sending his team away for a bit and seeking a solitary space for himself. This time was short-lived though, as the full moon shone bright on his team facing the challenge of a storm while at sea. Now, while there is some debate (based on the different Greek words used in this passage) over if Jesus truly walked on the water or not, one thing is for certain—when challenges arose, Jesus did not hesitate to join them in the chaos.[4] Once he arrived on the scene, brash Peter was the first to speak.

"Lord, if it's you," Peter replied, "tell me to come to you on the water."

"Come," he said.

Then Peter got down out of the boat, walked on the water and came toward Jesus. But when he saw the wind, he was afraid and, beginning to sink, cried out, "Lord, save me!"

Immediately Jesus reached out his hand and caught him. "You of little faith," he said, "why did you doubt?"

And when they climbed into the boat, the wind died down. Then those who were in the boat worshiped him, saying, "Truly you are the Son of God."

Now, let's use our educated imaginations a bit and create an inner-monologue for Peter, shall we?

---

4   Barclay; The Gospel of Matthew, 104.

The verses preceding this speaks to how the crowds *and* the disciples were distracted by their ideals of Jesus as a leader while being aloof to his words of carrying out the realities of heaven here and now. So perhaps Peter was thinking something along the lines of, "Let's see what you got, Jesus. Let's see if you are who you say you are. Let's see if you are more than an earthly ruler."

And as a gentle Savior who lovingly knew him, Jesus provided the requested information with the simple invite of, "Come."

Peter rushes into the water with confidence, "I *so* got this. I can lead in a way that Jesus wants me to, I can hang." He must have thought, while his belief in Jesus and himself carried him for a bit, his self-esteem and trajectory for success crumbled as self-doubt slipped in. "Oh, crud, this water can't hold me! I can't stand in this wind! Who am I to think I could actually answer Jesus's call? I can't do this! This is too much *for me!* Of course, I'm sinking. I was dumb to think I could ever have the courage or skill to do this (*Blub, blub, blub, garble*—insert gasping for air—because he's sinking)."

In moments of fear and uncertainty, it is difficult to avoid negative self-talk and self-doubt because stress chemicals (cortisol and adrenalin) are erupting in our brain that makes us operate out of survival mode. And what do we have to focus on in order to survive? Ourselves. And once we are in survival mode, our primitive brains are ready for danger, so all that we experience (including our thoughts) has a negative spin on it. [5]

One way to combat this natural reaction of the frazzled brain is through the practice of Mindfulness.

---

5   Wax, *A Mindfulness Guide for the Frazzled;* 64.

PLASTIC

"Mindfulness" is a huge buzzword right now in both the secular and spiritual teaching arenas. Although this practice is far from cutting-edge, new affirming research has rebirthed it. This therapeutic technique equips one to concentrate fully on the present moment.

In peacefully noticing and accepting one's thoughts and feelings, he can take ownership of these and guard them from the actions of others in the past or future. Some of the major benefits of this mental training include boosting the immune system, lowering the risk of heart disease, and decreasing one's symptoms of depression. Dr. Tina Payne-Bryson simplifies the practice of mindfulness as, "Paying attention on purpose", and studies suggest that we are at our happiest when we are doing exactly that.

Yes, we are the happiest when we are fully emotionally and mentally present. Yet, we are barely present for fifty-percent of our day, according to Matt Killingsworth's study. This software product manager designed an iPhone app that would randomly survey folks and ask them if, "they were thinking of something other than what they were currently doing?" He wanted to study happiness in correlation to how often our minds wander in the day. He received "650,000 surveys from 15,000 people, from a wide variety of countries, occupations, marital statuses, ages, and incomes." And he found that mind wandering was the cause of folk's unhappiness or (another way to say it) that folks are happiest when they are fully emotionally, and mentally present in the moment.[6] As with most things, the more we practice being mindful/being present, the easier it becomes.

---

6   Killingsworth, *Want to be Happier? Stay in the Moment.*

Although, mindfulness exercises can take the form of sculpting a symbol of one's day out of play dough or rediscovering one's grounded-ness while lying on the floor with soft music, one of the original forms was a lesser kinesthetic version—prayer. As one of London's leading voices in mental health, *The Mind & Soul Organization* teaches;

> "Within the Bible there is an implicit theology of attention and awareness. Jesus goes off very early in the morning to a solitary place to pray, which is an act of sustained attention (Mark 1:35). Peter and the disciples hunt him down and interrupt him, trying to distract him with what the crowd wants. Jesus switches his (and their) attention back to what really matters and says, 'Let us go somewhere else – to the nearby villages—so that I can preach there also. That is why I have come' (Mark 1:38)."

Not only is Jesus seen prioritizing stillness in the New Testament, but so are our Hebrew ancestors in the Old Testament. The prophet Elijah was striving to hear the voice of God, and while mistakenly thinking it would be heard in an earthquake or a fire, it was found in a still small voice in 1 Kings 19. As a compliment to the Biblical emphasis on solitude, neuroscientists and psychologists offer many helpful resources on the subject as well.

I would highly recommend the works of Ruby Wax, Tina Payne-Bryson and Dan Siegel. I also lean heavily on an app called Insight Timer to meet my mindfulness needs. In their (life-saving) work, mindfulness is taught to combat the "flight or fight" feeling that many experience while in stressful situations. They encourage you to rise above our distracted society that is lost in our competitive, comparative, and materialistic world. Learning to practice mindfulness also decreases one's negative self-talk and develops an overall perspective of contentment.

The more one practices mindfulness, the more neural pathways are created in the brain that helps her to more readily respond differently to stressful situations. Actually, studies suggest that some gray matter of the amygdala (the almond-shape cluster of neurons that is responsible for spewing out those nasty stress-hormones that lead to negative-self talk) decreases (since the brain is basically malleable plastic) overtime within those who practice mindfulness.[7]

Is that not unreal?!

Sometimes people assume that at a certain age, their brain stops growing and changing, but this could not be further from the truth. The brain is like plastic. It is *beyond* modifiable and changeable, as shown by one of the pioneers of modern brain science, Dr. Paul Bach-y-Rita in his study with his dad from the 1950s.

POET

His father Pedro (a Catalan scholar) had a stroke at sixty-five that left half of his body paralyzed, and left him unable to speak. After four weeks of rehab showed no improvements, Paul's brother, George, who was a medical doctor, took him in. Being clueless of the ways of rehabilitation, his ways were extremely unconventional. He had his dad crawl before he could learn to walk—with knee pads of course, and soon enough he could crawl beside walls. George shares on this experience,

"That crawling beside the wall went on for months. After that I even had him practicing in the garden, which led to problems with the neighbors, who were saying it wasn't nice, it was

---

7   Wax, *A Mindfulness Guide for the Frazzled;* 64-66.

unseemly, to be making the professor crawl like a dog. The only model I had was how babies learn. So we played games on the floor, with me rolling marbles, and him having to catch them. Or we'd throw coins on the floor, and he'd have to try and pick them up with his weak right hand. Everything we tried involved turning normal life experiences into exercises."[8]

After several weeks, Pedro was able to walk and stand. After three months of working on speech, Pedro was able to make a few sounds and relearned how to write, and, in time, he learned how to use a typewriter again. By the time a year had passed, Pedro was back to teaching again and taught for five more years until he retired.

Seven years after his stroke, while hiking the peaks of Columbia, he passed away from a heart attack. While looking at the slides of his father's autopsy, Paul shared these mind-blowing discoveries.

> "What the slides showed was that my father had had a huge lesion from his stroke and that it had never healed, even though he recovered all those functions. I freaked out. I got numb. I was thinking, 'Look at all this damage he has...How can you recover with all this damage?' The lesion was mainly in the brain stem—the part of the brain closest to the spinal cord—and the other major brain centers in the cortex that control movement had been destroyed by the stroke as well. Ninety-seven percent of the nerves that run from the cerebral cortex to the spine were destroyed—catastrophic damage that had caused his paralysis. I knew that meant that somehow his brain had totally reorganized itself."[9]

The discovery that the brain has the power to rearrange itself based on one's thoughts and actions was not only a huge game

---

8   Doidge, *The Brain That Changes Itself*, 21.

9   Ibid., 23.

changer for the world of neuroscience, but it also led to Bach-y-Rita switching gigs and focusing strictly on brain research.

Is that not mind-blowing? Or should I say, mind-changing?! As Victor Copan unpacks this Pedro study further, "What we *do* with our bodies and what we *think* with our minds *literally* changes the structure of our brains"[10] and practices like mindfulness can assist in *reshaping* our brains in the healthiest of ways possible.

So, in time that mistake that used to make you think, "Oh, crap! I'm such a moron! How could I let that happen?!" soon leads to a much kinder reaction of, "OK. That was not ideal, but it will only take ten-ish minutes to correct and next time I will be more careful," because of you being more mindful of your thoughts and self-talk. (Not to mention, if you're not making mistakes, you're probably not being innovative enough.)

Through mindfulness, we accept that we cannot always control our surroundings or the *actions and feelings* of others, but we can take control of *our* reactions to these. In pausing for a moment of solitude, in making a point to "pay attention on purpose," we can tap into the sense of peace, strength, and affirmation that only the Holy Spirit who dwells within can provide and begin to see ourselves and the situation as God does.

Like some friends share, being kind to oneself and maintaining grit during the contrary winds of life is possible no matter if one is:

- Getting fired from a job during a workforce reduction like Roy who told himself, "Don't take this personally, and separate yourself from the emotion of betrayal and stay focused on getting another job."

10   Copan, *Changing the Mind*, 90.

- Being raised by a mom who is incapable of comforting and nurturing her like Chandelle who started telling herself, "I will focus on my own strength, my own self-love and my future beyond my childhood home."

- Forced to alter how she does her job like Nora and started practicing the self-talk of, "There has to be some way to make this new reality work. I have to figure out the silver linings, no matter how small they are. I must find a new focus that keeps me motivated and excited. I will ask for help."

- Dealing with chronic pain like Allen, who daily says, "I can't do this, but with God all things are possible. I can do anything through Christ."

- Or like Eliza who left a job and community she loved for a new gig in a state she had only visited before who practiced such mantras as, "God has called me to this. I am well-suited for this work. I will make friends. I have what it takes to make the best situation out of this."

NEANDERTHAL

And this type of self-talk is just what the doctor (and life-coach) ordered to help us not be screwed over by our brains—our brains that still react in *very* primal ways, especially under stress.

For example, as Mel Robbins teaches, procrastination is not related to your work ethic or attitude but a survival technique that goes back to our cave(wo)man days. It's never the task that we are avoiding but the stress that we are connecting with said task. What is now the grumpiness of the DMV clerk, was once

94

some prehistoric cat just a-waitin' to pounce while you hunted for brunch.

In maintaining positive self-talk, I'm keeping my brain calm so I can explore the cause of the stress that I am associating with a specific task. I can analyze if, "The stress is coming from a real threat or a perceived one. Or what's the worst-case scenario that [I'm] fearful of?" [11]

When I ask myself these questions in a perceived stressful situation, I get a much clearer image of what it is I am working with, and it's way less intimidating. These questions lead me to the discovery that in all actuality this disturbance of a task will only take thirty-minutes (For me, stating out loud how much of my life a task will steal in minutes, makes me more apt to do it), and the impact it will have on my life *if* I fail will be less than minor. One-hundred percent of the time, when I visualize the worst possible outcome of a task that I am putting off, I grasp that I still come out alive, most likely with a few lessons learned.

Not only is our mind prone to procrastinate at the sight of (perceived) stress, but it's also wired to not like risks, even the most fun and creative ones. (You're a real buzz-kill, mind.) It prefers to remain in auto-pilot mode, and at the first instinctual nudge (gut–reaction) we get towards an idea, after five-seconds our mind will begin "telling" us all of the reasons we should not walk towards the attractive person at the party or apply for that new position.

So what do we do?

---

11   Koulopoulos, *Science Says This 5-Second Rule Will Make Your Brain Stop Procrastinating.*

We tell ourselves that we are waiting for the "right time" to chase after a goal, but the truth is that the "right time" will never come.

Why won't the "right time" ever come? Well, in her book, *The Five Second Rule*, Mel Robbins explains that this is because: 1) Change is always new; 2) It always comes with uncertainty; and 3) It's always scary. So we accept these and to rise above them, she teaches that we must complete small tasks towards a goal within the *first* five seconds of being nudged towards it. With this, the feelings of procrastination or feared failure will fade away and, from each small act of courage, more courage follows.

A task can be as simple as writing an idea down on a napkin, laying out running shoes the night before or literally putting one foot in front of the other towards that hottie at the party, and when we physically *do,* neurological magic happens. As addressed earlier, a huge chunk of information processing occurs in our stomach *long* before it reaches our brains and we put words to it. Robbins calls these moments when we trust our gut "decisions of courage," and by avoiding the "habit of hesitation" and executing these choices one small step at a time, we are saving our mind from getting lost in the ruminating realm of self-doubt and fictitious, futuristic fears.

Sadly during moments of stress and self-abasing talk (same thing) the part of our brain which guides our steps to a goal, the prefrontal cortex, shuts down due to all of the stress hormones that are shooting up from the amygdala (as addressed before); therefore, by simply taking one step (no matter how small) towards your gut-nudged goal, you are shifting gears in your brain like one does in a car, and reactivating the prefrontal cortex.

You are forbidding your primal brain to screw you over.

And by acting on a decision one step at a time, you are not only confronting the stress, but you are setting up your brain to match the processing pace of your fast-acting gut. In time it will be easier to move towards goals without any procrastination or negative self-talk.

I watched Mel Robbin's TED talk over her "Five Second Rule" and immediately began writing my first book. She *totally* shifted how I view my mind and my creative process. When it was published I sent her a copy and a thank you note, for if it were not for her work, that book (or this one) wouldn't exist. Whenever anyone asks me for advice on writing a book, the first thing I do is send them her TED talk with a note that reads, "Before you type any word, you must first set your mind up for success."

PLATTER

Another way to set your mind up for success is to assure it's as balanced as possible, and balance is relative to each person. Regardless, a balanced mind, as Dan Siegel and David Rock teach, not only optimizes brain matter, but it also enhances one's well-being. To help one in exploring what a balanced mind would look like for her, they created the Healthy Mind Platter [12] which serves up seven essential mental activities in her day.

Depending on one's temperament, some of us may desire more or less of each of these, but we require all of them. In order to be our best selves and reach those beloved goals of ours we must make time for:

---

12   Siegel, *Healthy Mind Platter.*

- **Focus time:** When we closely focus on tasks in a goal-oriented way, we take on challenges that make deep connections in the brain.

- **Play time:** When we allow ourselves to be spontaneous or creative, playfully enjoying novel experience, we help make new connections in the brain.

- **Connecting time:** When we connect with other people, ideally in person (sorry, *Instagram*) and when we take time to appreciate our connection to the natural world around us, we activate and reinforce the brain's relational circuitry.

- **Physical time:** When we move our bodies, aerobically if medically possible, we strengthen the brain in many ways.

- **Time in:** When we quietly reflect internally, focusing on sensations, images, feelings, and thoughts, we help to better integrate the brain.

- **Down time:** When we are non-focused, without any specific goal, and let our mind wander or simply relax, we help the brain recharge.

- **Sleep time:** When we give the brain the rest it needs, we consolidate learning and recover from the experiences of the day.

Similar to the USDA's "choose my plate" image, these seven things make up "mental nourishment" and the desired slices of each will vary from person to person. Chances are if you often struggle with procrastination or self-abasing talk, you're not enjoying a Healthy Mind Platter each day.

Discovering what my own Healthy Mind Platter looks like has taken me some time, so hopefully reading this part of the book will save you some. Thankfully, I had a mom who was addicted to therapy, so a few counselors helped me along the way.

As I shared on previous pages, I am slightly obsessed with personality tests, and the only one that helped me more than the enneagram over the years is the work by Carol Tuttle in *Living Your Truth.* (If you are friends, with Carol, please don't tell her that I referred to her work as a personality test, for she would be highly offended.) Along with counselors, her work has helped to greatly decrease my anxiety (and the accompanying hives and ulcers) and increase my creativity, focus, and empathy.

Thanks to these steps, I confidently map my mind in the following ways to assure my utmost well-being. Basically if my day is filled with movement, goals obtained, and conversations, I am as content as a clam! My limit of introspective time is three hours (no more!) a day, and I honestly need those to be successful on all levels. And whenever my fear and negative self-talk are through the roof, I *know* it's because I haven't been giving my mind the unique nourishment that it needs. All this to say, the state of my emotional health has *very* little to do with other's choices, and *everything* to do with honoring how I'm wired in mine.

Thankfully, I married a man with different needs than mine, and from him I have learned the importance of rest and play. It has been quite lovely over the years to learn from his opposite needs of more 'time in' and less 'physical time.' He has naturally helped me to have a well-rounded mind platter. This will be unpacked further on later pages, but if I hadn't swept him off his feet, I would be a burnt-out workaholic with no friends for miles. #truth

Carol Tuttle writes about each of us having different energy types and she beautifully compares these types to parts of creation. I have the determined, swift energy of Niagara Falls, where as Garrett has the methodical, subtle nature of a weeping willow tree. Like in nature, both of these movements/energy types are equally beautiful and necessary. They are not judged, nor is one deemed as better than the other. All energy types are respected in the great outdoors, and it would behoove us to appreciate these uniquenesses in others' mental wiring as well.

The more I studied about the brain and personality differences, the more empathy I had for my most uptight, high-maintenance parishioners. Once I realized that the very grumpy stay-at-home mom had not left her home or her two children for three days as she was yelling at me, it was easier for me to offer her grace. No wonder she was stressed and using my lack of hand-sanitizer while cooking for the community meal as her punching bag; her brain was not being nourished with a well-rounded platter each day. She was not honoring how her brain was uniquely wired. Out of the seven essentials that her mind needed, she was only getting one or two: play and *some* sleep.

SIDE SERMON #1

(Side sermon: It always makes me chuckle when frazzled stay-at-home-parents have confused their need for a break from their kids as their *identity* as a staunch introvert.

"I'm an introvert! I'm an introvert!" They tell everyone for miles at an awkwardly loud volume.

Introverts don't interrupt or seek to steer conversations, Patrice. You're just a stressed-out extrovert who desperately needs adult conversation and intellectual challenges. And actually, chances are you'd feel even more off-kilter if you had more time alone.

So please, for the sake of everyone in this meeting, would you (FOR THE LOVE OF ALL THINGS HOLY) join a book club, rec class or SOMETHING that meets your extrovert needs and stop using these meetings as your weekly social hour? Got it? Good. Now, if you're done highjacking this meeting, I would love to get back to the agenda, you dear soft, subtle, reserved "introvert" who never stops talking.)

Taking the time to figure out how your mind is wired and *honoring* this (through your surroundings and tasks) will significantly set you up for not only mental success, but emotional success as well. As the neuroscientists, Antonio Damasio teaches in his book, *Descartes' Error,* 95% of our decisions are ultimately decided by *feelings*, not facts. (Remember the gut-reaction we talked about?) He, therefore, calls us, "feeling machines that think, not thinking machines that feel." And on that note, it's time for things to get a little touchy-feely.

I am my own sanctuary.

Because I house the Holy, grit and grace come from within, regardless of the choices of others.

My body is beautiful;
a gift that should be cared for,
trusted, and never feared.

My mind is uniquely mine.
While it is ever-expanding,
I call the shots on its focus,
stillness, and creativity.

AS YOU FORGE ONWARD AS YOUR OWN SANCTUARY, ASK YOURSELF:

What personal daily Mind Platter is needed to best set you up for mental success? Remember like Dan Siegal teaches, your platter might look differently than others in your life. How many hours of each do *you* require? Is this different than what you are currently getting? What is one step you can take this week to serve yourself up *exactly* what you need? Write your ideal ways to spend in each of these categories.

1. **Focus time:** *When we closely focus on tasks in a goal-oriented way, we take on challenges that make deep connections in the brain.*

2. **Play time:** *When we allow ourselves to be spontaneous or creative, playfully enjoying novel experience, we help make new connections in the brain.*

3. **Connecting time:** *When we connect with other people, ideally in person (sorry, Instagram) and when we take time to appreciate our connection to the natural world around us, we activate and reinforce the brain's relational circuitry.*

4. **Physical time:** *When we move our bodies, aerobically if medically possible, we strengthen the brain in many ways.*

5. **Time in:** *When we quietly reflect internally, focusing on sensations, images, feelings, and thoughts, we help to better integrate the brain.*

6. **Down time:** *When we are non-focused, without any specific goal, and let our mind wander or simply relax, we help the brain recharge.*

7. **Sleep time:** *When we give the brain the rest it needs, we consolidate learning and recover from the experiences of the day*

CHAPTER FOUR

Embracing My Emotions: Jesus and All the Feelings

Have you ever been so ticked off at work that you just *Office Spaced* it?

Ya know, ya just stopped caring and then left (minus the hypnosis and the gutting of the fish)?

I have.

Yep, just once, but I've done it. Right in the middle of a meeting, I gathered up my things and left.

I. Was. Livid.

Even my kind boss tried to stop me, but I wasn't having it. I was so livid that I couldn't even speak, which is rare for me (clearly).

While the words were not coming, the mad tears didn't hold back, and that blasted new tinge in my forehead that I shared earlier on returned. After crying to my husband over the phone, I simply didn't want to be alone with my anger. So, I went to a friend's office and cried some more. She had a meeting, so my wailing was short-lived. Upon our goodbyes, I did the only thing a happy-go-lucky-high-energy-extrovert-who's-used-to-repressing-unattractive-emotions does with the weight of this still foreign feeling—I went to the gym.

Once there, I ran intervals for over two hours on the treadmill while watching a Bryan Cranston comedy that was so far from funny that I won't even plug it. (Sorry, Bryan, although I do still love your work with *Sneaky Pete*.) A little after the two-hour mark, I realized that the endorphin rush was not only good for my mood, but that I had most likely reached such a point of dehydration that I had no more tears left to cry.

Mission accomplished.

While I thought my gym trip would quiet my anger, it didn't. It turns out my anger had *lots* of opinions. I tried not to give it too much of a voice by dwelling or venting, because that would be giving it more life. In fact, studies suggests that the same neurological occurrence takes place when the event is remembered as when it actually occurred. (To your brain, there is no difference.) And I saw no good in putting the most pissed-off I've ever been on instant replay—I mean ruminating was something I already came by naturally. So, I tried to ignore my anger, but it would not be silenced.

MEAN GIRLS/SIDE SERMON #2

It was in this moment, and I offer no apologies for this side sermon, that I realized how tricky emotions can be for women in leadership. And this was somewhat new for me, for on the majority of personality assessments I take (because of my addiction to them), my results lean more towards the qualities that we in the US would label as 'masculine.' I have also thankfully *never* felt looked upon any differently because of my gender. In fact, the rare times (including this crap-show) that another threw shade at me for being a working mom in a leadership position came from other women, *not* my male teammates.

And side-sermon-inside-a-sermon: if we *ever* want to achieve equality among the genders, and make the world a more peaceful place, we women have to learn to be nicer to each other. As the real Queen B, Tina Fey (Ms. Norbury) said in the film *Mean Girls*, "…you all have *got* to stop calling each other sluts and whores. It just makes it OK for guys to call you sluts and whores." Now while we small-town, mini-van moms don't call each other these exact words, what we say about those who choose vaccines, family beds, and daycare can be *just* as harmful, if not worse.

Seriously.

Moms-who-work-outside-of-the-home (What is it? 1964?), it's *OK* to love your job and your kids. It's more than OK, go ahead and love the heck out of both of them. Tell that neurotic guilt to shut the flip up! (I tear up as I type these words, which means I have some fragments of misplaced-guilt floating around from the mommy-shamming.)

It. Is. OK. You go, you world-changer, you dreamer-of-dreams! You, go, Momma! God wouldn't call you to the work without the promise of providing for you and your family as you serve.

Answer that calling! God's got you!

GOD'S GOT YOU!

Stay-at-home-Moms, please be nicer to moms who felt called to "raise kids and dreams"[1] within the *same* life-season.

And moms who work outside of the home, we *mustn't* look down on stay-at-home-moms (or dads) if they have chosen to

---

1   A line by blogger, Michayla White.

work solely inside of the home; for many *often* work just as hard (if not harder) and it's simply a *different* type of work. Not only are there different types of work, but more importantly, there are different types of healthy families.

Can I get an amen?!

There are healthy kids who homeschool (Yeah, I made that a verb.) who eat *only* organic veggies, only see their siblings, and don't watch TV. Equally true, there are healthy kids who eat Pop-Tarts and watch *Trolls* on the way to pre-school where fifteen "best friends" await them.

All of us have the right to build the life for our families to which we have been called, and mommy-shaming solves *nothing* and causes premature aging. So STOP IT! #Merica

It really grinds my gears (if it is not already clear) that our gender is known for not being able to work well together.

Shit.

Nothing ticks me off more in a conversation of a failed business when someone ignorantly says, "but that's just how it is when a group of women try to work together. It's tough, all that malicious gossiping and cowardly backstabbing."

Bull corn.

Nope. I refuse to accept that as truth.

It does not have to be tough. We can learn not to be jealous of each other's different life-paths and talents. We can learn to celebrate diversity. We can decline the invite to the eternal competition of weight and style. We can learn to speak honestly to one another. We can grow in our emotional maturity and not throw shade because we hate our own lives so much and she seems so happy with her goals. We can become so self-aware that we can decipher when our emotions need to take the lead, and when they need to take a back-seat. And we can expand our lens and not hold her to a flipping different standard than a man in the workplace. (Take it from one who is basically a very curvy man by most personality tests.)

Side sermon over.

Now, where was I? (Isn't this a fun adventure everyone?)

Oh yeah, the day I left work ticked-off and realized that my anger, like me, was extremely long-winded.

I became keenly aware of the different expectations that were put on me as a woman when it came to dealing with my "anger," and for guidance, I reached out to my mom.

As one who *aggressively* climbed the ladder to the position of Assistant Superintendent for a school district, her advice was to, "not show any emotion at all when confronting this, stick to the facts, apologize only for what needs to be apologized for and get to sharing your solution to the problem as *quickly* as possible. Get in and get out. Don't over talk it, Meg. Don't give them too much of your time. Don't give them too much power." Boom, just like that.

Compare this to my top-tier friend[2] Lindsay, who was extremely successful in her career at a college as well as a stay-at-home-parent, who said, "I don't know, Meg. I love your mom, but she was raised in a different time than we female leaders of today. As she paved the way for all of us, she and others had to remain emotionless to succeed, and I think our generation is different. We can be vulnerable, and we can authentically speak to our feelings. They need to know that they hurt you, Meg. That is the only way that teams can heal and move forward. Plus, you have been with them so long, that you can go deep with them.

---

2   A line made famous by Mindy Kaling.

I hate to go against your Mom's advice and all, but I don't think you will gain *anything* by repressing your emotions here."

Being slightly intimidated by both of their wise routes, I stalled and did nothing. #LikeABoss

NICKI MINAJ

And after a day or two, I was convinced that my anger couldn't/ shouldn't be ignored, so I tapped into it and wrote a poem. What I expected to be a poised Dickinson-like poem, turned out to not be a poem at all; well not a traditional poem. It was a poem with a beat. It was a rap. Yep, who my anger sounded like once I finally gave it a microphone was Nicki Minaj. It was raw, articulate, hopeful, but overall—downright pissed.

Ok, Anger, Listen Up.

OK, anger you can stay, but you don't call the shots today.
I'll get in my car, drive away, find my confidence in *Beyoncé.*

OK, anger you have fought, but my soul you will not rot.
Perched at my desk, emotionless rock,
acting resilient, when I am not.

OK, anger...

OK, anger, ok....

OK, *anger.* Yeah—I get it.

OK, ANGER, I SAID OK!

You listen to *me*! Go ahead and get comfy,
for it's *my* turn to speak.

110

I won't ignore you, you're my data, *not* my direction[3].
But with my heated state, convos take strict selection.

Yes, I hear their words on constant replay,
like the end of a VHS, loud, fuzzy dots on display.

In the big scheme of things, "this" does not matter,
but in this moment, my joy's been shattered.

Why didn't she protect me? Why didn't he fight?
Got me poppin' melatonin to ease my mind at night.

Their assumptions, right-hooks; Their doubt, a headlock
Is my reputation and character worth the chopping block?

Mistakes of the under-performing? Sugar-coated, denounced.
A misconstrued sight of *my* "flaw"? And all will pounce.

When building a team, your best set the bar,
They'll create the culture, hold the rest to par.

Alas, I'm powerless to the systemic issues here.
But, amygdala, calm down and Peace, draw near.

Anger.....leave!

I'm done dancing to what you sing.
I will now seek the good that God *will* bring.

It was only after this poem that I was able to speak honestly
to the persons who had caused my anger, and thankfully this
led to some restoration. I am grateful that I gave my anger the

---

3   A line made famous by Susan David.

microphone of the rap, the soothing caress of loved ones, and the ring of the treadmill.

All in all, I'm just plain thankful that I had reached a healthy enough place in which I *allowed* myself to *feel* anger—to feel heartache—and (even better) to properly name it as such to those who had caused it.

NED FLANDERS-SYNDROME

For many years I, like other holy-rollers, suffered from my self-diagnosis of "Ned-Flanders-Syndrome." Named after Homer Simpson's overly-positive, churchaholic neighbor, some are incapable of feeling any (wrongfully labeled) negative emotions for fear that these might display a weak faith. How could we possibly feel discontent or angry with the high amounts of joy, joy, joy down in our hearts (down in our hearts)?

So, we repress, we deny, and we sugar coat lots of things to *ourselves* and others. And to add to the awkwardness that is Ned-Flanders-Syndrome, ministers are often afraid to show too much emotion towards *anything*, as fear that this would break a professional boundary. In turn, we come off as socially forced in many of our interactions.

While we should not fear them (any of them), we should not ignore them either. Instead, as Dr. Susan David teaches in her book, *Emotional Agility*, we should learn to look at most emotions as data as opposed to direction. What values do our feelings about a certain situation reveal? When my daughter started preschool, I learned to give myself grace about the amount of fear that was welling up within me; for this fear represented that I valued her safety and overall development.

These are admirable values, and it would be hard for one to be a good parent without them. Now, should I have followed these feelings as direction? And not enrolled her? No, for these specific feelings were not direction, they were simply pieces of data that were reminding me of my principles. Even though I was worried about this milestone, the facts were that Henley *was* ready (on all cylinders) for pre-school. As an only child, the peer interaction was necessary. It was a stellar preschool, and she basically came out of the womb asking to go to school. She. Was. Ready. And these facts beautifully aligned with the value that my fear reminded me of, so we enrolled her and it was an amazing success. (Plus, even the staunchest homeschooling mom will tell you (as she did me) that fear is not the right motive for keeping a child at home.

Emotions are not only good, but they were initially created to ensure our survival. While some days it may seem like your emotions are manipulating, they really *do* mean well (most days). As the amazing Ruby Wax shares, "We first pick up their scent in our bodies, created by various cocktails of chemicals that provide us with moment-to-moment feedback on what to avoid and what to approach. To avoid danger, a weasel sniffs the wind, a snail ups its antennae, an octopus extends a tentacle, while we humans use our emotions to test the waters."[4] Our emotions are a divinely given gift that help us to determine what is safe or unsafe for us.

Thousands more emotions exist than what we can verbally translate; for our finite language is at times insufficient in its capabilities. (Shocking to all extroverts, yeah?!)

---

4   Wax; *How to Be Human*, 46.

Sure, we can try, but we in no way will be describing all that we are feeling. This might surprise you, but emotions come before our thoughts. As we learned earlier from Mel Robbins, we feel first and think second. It's a quick, less than a second transfer from feeling to thought, but nonetheless, the emotion *is* leading the way. This powerful first response is the result of a neuro-chemical system that grants us a sense of not only our values, but our physical beings as well.

All of our emotions served a purpose as we look back over our ancestral story. In our primitive days, rage helped us to scare off our enemy. Anxiety, remembering past similar events, ensured we were prepared for attacks or moves. Disgust made sure we would not consume of anything poisonous, and our facial reactions would warn our tribe members. Even the grimy feeling of shame served a much healthier purpose yonder back. It used to deal with our role as a valuable member of our tribe, and our tribe was *everything* to us. It was not as neurotic as shame is today, for it was *not* about *us*. (Shut the front door!) If we sensed we had let our tribe down, shame would motivate us to work harder or do better to better benefit the group.[5]

Many moons ago, before we were isolated, frazzled beings who averaged around seven hours of screen time a day, it was much easier to recognize our emotions and use them in healthier ways. It's a totally different story now, and Wax assures us that in 2020 stress-related illnesses will be the leading cause of death. She (as one with clinical depression) also goes as far as to point out that while clinical depression and anxiety *do* exist, many of us do not have these conditions, but simply have some of their symptoms due to our frazzled lifestyles.

---

5   Ibid, 48-49.

Why are we so stressed?

We are overwhelmed by choices, work, and our schedules are too full. We're overly caffeinated, sleep-deprived humans who need to do less, *but* move more. Furthermore, since the invention of language, once our brains are in a stressed-out state, (Remember the flood of stress hormones to the brain from the last chapter?) our brains tend to stress about stress, and in some cases we ruminate.[6]

PINK ELEPHANTS

Not everyone ruminates, but I am one of the chosen who has had the "privilege."

"Rumination refers to the tendency to *repetitively* think about the causes, situational factors, and consequences of one's negative emotional experience. Basically, rumination means that you continuously think about the various aspects of situations that are upsetting."[7] And you *can't* turn it off. It's a nasty gnawing narrative that can skew perceptions of reality.

Once the brain does it once with a certain subject matter, it naturally wants to do it again, because as Tina Payne-Bryson teaches (for better or for worse), "Whatever neurons fire get wired." This is specifically true in high-stress situations. Or as Wax writes, "We all have specific fear triggers embedded in our memories which we react to emotionally without knowing why, especially when in a tense situation. We're at the mercy of old associations." [8]

---

6   Wax; *A Mindfulness Guide for the Frazzled*, 14-33.

7   Selby; *Rumination: Problem Solving Gone Wrong*.

8   Wax; *How to Be Human*, 51.

I recall first ruminating as a seventh grader.

With my dad fighting in the Bosnian conflict, my parents being separated and us living with my grandparents, my brain was a busted fire hydrant of nasty stress hormones. Thankfully, my mom's addiction to therapy paid off and a counselor, without using the term 'rumination', helped me to understand what was occurring in my brain.

He encouraged me to protect my over-worried, overly-creative, overly-imaginative mind from potentially frightening influences. He shared with me in a very diplomatic, half-truth kind of way (as my Mom pulled a Beverly Goldberg and hovered) that the more imaginative/creative one is, the more prone she is to ruminate.

"What do you think about, Meg, when I tell you *not* to think about pink elephants?"

He said.

"Nothing but pink elephants." I said.

"Exactly. It's for this reason that when you feel these intrusive thoughts taking over your brain, you shouldn't try to turn them off by telling yourself *not* to think about them. Don't fight them; for in fighting them you increase their volume. Simply notice that they are there, but don't give into them and know that they're not your reality." He shared while jotting down notes on his pad.

This therapy session was super-helpful, but it didn't stop the ruminating. I still had episodes. I would tell my teen self when they happened, "You're not crazy. You're just stressed. Try to focus on something else." And by college I had figured out my own tactic to deal with them. I figured out that I was more likely to ruminate if I had gone too long without movement, intellectual challenges, or conversations. (Remember Mind Mapping? I learned how to set myself up for emotional success.) However, during high stress-situations, my mind would flirt with ruminating more naturally (obviously).

My self-created tactic for dealing with rumination was that I would focus on an inanimate object, and I would start spelling it backwards. If I saw a chair, I would say inside my head, "r-i-a-h-c." I would simply breathe and spell, breathe and spell. And I would do this until I was brought back into the present moment. If you've ever ruminated before, you know that it's *heavier* than a thought. It's an undeniable sensation whenever an episode of rumination is lurking. I feel it throughout my entire being.

Twenty years after the pink-elephant talk, another counselor defined rumination for me. It was such a relief to know that it was common enough to have a name. It totally normalized it for me. She was such a skilled counselor that she helped me to differentiate the sensations of ruminating thoughts (which are *not* my reality) and thoughts that *were* my reality.

Ruby Wax teaches us that some mental events (that we confuse as thoughts) are simply like dark storm clouds in the distance.

We notice them floating in the distance, but we don't run from them and at the *same time*, we don't accept them as our reality. We just take note that they are there, that they are most likely signs of some nasty stress hormones doing weird things in our brain, but we are *not* those thoughts, and they are not us.

However, twelve years before meeting that skilled counselor, I knew *very* little about how the brain worked, and I figured that what my backwards bit might be doing was switching from my right brain to the left. But what I was really doing, unbeknownst to me, was practicing a form of mindfulness and switching the gears of my brain (like in a car). And since our thoughts and feelings work together, we're going to bring the brain back into the conversation.

Once a moment of rumination begins, it is an endless cycle of anxious thoughts to feelings to thoughts to feelings. The brain is sending stressful messages to the body and the body back to the brain. It's endless! With this said, trying to stop that cycle by using the prefrontal-cortex where the action is mainly taking place (although other parts are playing a role) and *telling* yourself to stop thinking about it will be useless. So, what do you do? The cycle can't be stopped from inside of the cycle!

By working outside of a ruminating cycle, you are able to end it. When your inner-dialogue is stuck in a dark loop, you can't use language to stop the loop. You got to get outside of that loop. Tap into your senses (touch, sight, etc.,), and in doing so, you switch gears in your brain. With this, the amygdala calms down and ceases its spraying of those nasty stress hormones (which add to the rumination) and you are able to observe and, eventually, *end* the negative-thought-cycle from *outside* of the cycle. Our brains are so amazing that the pre-frontal cortex allows us to *think* about thinking.

I accomplished this by tapping into my sense of sight, spelling ten-to-fifteen words backwards, and breathing. Yes, even in seminary, dropping a loved-one off at rehab, and a high-risk pregnancy, this little strategy of my teen years helped every time. (Although, my episodes are few and far between these days thanks to Mind Mapping.) And if you read the mindfulness exercises from the professionals, you will see that (somehow) my strategy is very similar.

When we stress about stress (or for some, when we take this to the next level and ruminate for too long) crazy-bad things happen to us physically. Wax teaches that:

"The first thing to go down will be your memory, then your immune, digestive, and reproductive systems…This is all happening under your radar so you won't be aware that your system is deteriorating or why your brain cells are beginning to atrophy. Trust me on this, we all have myelin sheaths that cover each of your nerve cells (neurons) to speed up their signals to each other. If those sheaths get damaged, the neurons connecting different regions of the brain get weaker and the result is you can no longer put your thoughts together and your ability to be rational goes AWOL. In effect, you've been dumbed down."[9]

Without the ability to think straight, we start to feel threatened, and what was once just feeling "a lil' stressed," has now left us paranoid about our relationships. Some (not implying myself here *at all*) might become super competitive in all areas of my—I mean his—life during such neuronal atrophy. Even worse than endlessly being on the defense is when one starts to view anyone who is different as the enemy (which sadly, many do).

The saddest part about some of our reactions to being emotionally triggered is that very rarely can we pinpoint why our brain just gave us a shot of a nasty stress hormone, or why our stomach just got tight at the scent of that man's cologne. Yes, remember our gut *can* be more of an information processer than our brain (it has more neurons after all). But then again, there are moments when we don't perceive something truthfully. We perceive it, Wax teaches, "through the *interpretation* of our own memories."[10]

(Do you remember me already sharing that fact on earlier pages? What is your memory of me sharing that with you? Complimentary test.)

---

9   Wax; *How to Be Human,* 51.

10   Ibid, 52.

Did you catch that? We don't perceive/remember things necessarily on what factually occurred in our past but on our *interpretation* of that memory. More refreshing than that, each time our brain replays a memory, it's not replaying the situation itself but the *last* version that we played in our minds—which most likely has morphed a bit since he called you fat on the court in '96.

Think of how this affects our relationships with others, especially when a chance comes to forgive. Think of how much better we could operate if we were aware enough to decipher which emotions were *worth* trusting and which were simply to be viewed as dark storm clouds in the distance.

Since these moments do not point to our values or our reality, we accept them as the whacky squirts of stress-hormones that they are and let them float on. (Float on by you clouds of past regrets! Get gone, you clouds of future fictitious fantasies! Get!)

In this acceptance, we are not tempted to fight or run from them. On the other hand, with our emotions that are in line with our values; with those emotions that emerge from being fully present in a moment, we say, "Welcome. I'm listening. What do you have to teach me?" There's no such thing as an 'unhealthy' emotion. All emotions should be welcomed and no one exemplified this more than Jesus.

OVERTURNED TABLES

All throughout the gospels, He was able to stay in touch with and express His emotions with an unabashed freedom. As one who was fully human, He experienced the full range of human emotion, and He did so deeply. We note that Jesus:

- **Felt fear**—Matthew 26:39 "Father, if it is possible, let this cup away from me."

- **Felt sorry for people**—Luke 7:13 "When the Lord saw her, He felt compassion for her, and said to her, "Do not weep.""

- **Was moved with pity**—Mark 1:41 "moved with compassion, Jesus stretched out His hand..."

- **Felt anger**—Matthew 21:12-13 "Jesus entered the temple courts and drove out all who were buying and selling there. He overturned the tables of the money changers and the benches of those selling doves."

- **Knew longing, yearning, sorrow, and disappointment**—Luke 13:34 "Jerusalem, Jerusalem, you who kill the prophets and stone those sent to you, how often I have longed to gather your children together, as a hen gathers her chicks under her wings, and you were not willing."

- **Felt sadness**—Matthew 26:37 "He took Peter and the two sons of Zebedee along with him, and he began to be sorrowful and troubled."

- **Grieved**— Mark 3:5 "to find the people so obstinate, and looked *angrily* around."

- **Could be indignant**—Mark 10:14 "When Jesus saw this, he was indignant. He said to them, "Let the little children come to me...""

- **Was sometimes filled with joy**—Luke 10:21 "At that time Jesus, full of joy through the Holy Spirit, said, "I praise you, Father...""

- **Felt gratitude**—John 11:42 "Before calling Lazarus forth from the tomb: "Father, I thank you for having heard me…"

- **Shed tears**—Luke 19:41 "As he approached Jerusalem and saw the city, he wept over it." and John 11:35 "Jesus wept."

- **Was sometimes amazed and astonished**—Matthew 8:10 "When Jesus heard this, he was amazed and said to those following him, "truly I tell you, I have not found anyone in Israel with such great faith."

It was on the stage of relationships that his emotions danced. Jesus had close friendships with Martha and Lazarus (John 11:5); Mary Magdalene (Mark 16:1-11, Luke 24:1-11, Matthew 28:1-10, John 20:1-18); and his core three of Peter, James, and John (Matthew 17:1–8, Mark 9:2–8, Luke 9:28–36). At the same time, I bet he occasionally wanted to establish a healthy avoidance of the Pharisees (John 2:15-16) and lawyers (Luke 10:25-27) when they angered/annoyed him.

All of our emotions, even those deemed as "unattractive", serve a purpose in our relationships with our self and others.

Rage helps us to take a stand against that which is harmful to us or others. It can also help us to teach others how to treat us when we have been mistreated. Finally, it can be a firm motivator for holding a loved one accountable to his/her best self.

Anxiety helps us to remember past similar events, and to be more prepared for the future.

Jealousy could be reminding *you* of a desired goal that you haven't made time to chase.

Fear and sadness, like other emotions, point strongly toward our greatest values and loves.

Shame (when it is healthy and not neurotic) can motivate us to improve our actions for the betterment of ourselves and others.

Let's turn the page now to explore the greatest goal of one's spirit: to be in authentic relationships.

I am my own sanctuary.

My being houses the Holy. Grit
and grace come from within,
regardless of the choices of others.

My body is beautiful;
a gift that should be cared for,
trusted, and never feared.

My mind is uniquely mine.
While it is ever-expanding,
I call the shots on its focus,
stillness, and creativity.

My emotions are all necessary and should be embraced.

AS YOU FORGE ONWARD AS YOUR OWN SANCTUARY, ASK YOURSELF:

1. What emotion is difficult for you to embrace? When was the last time this emotion revealed itself? What about this emotion makes it uncomfortable for you?

2. How do you think Jesus's life, ministry, and influence would have been different if he hadn't experienced the full range of human emotions?

3. If you have a mind that is prone to ruminate, how would you describe the difference between the thoughts that *are* your reality and anxious, "storm clouds in the distance" thoughts birthed from the negative thought-cycle? Do they bring about different physiological sensations to you? (Nothing helped decrease my rumination habit more than Ruby Wax's, *The Mindfulness Guide for The Frazzled*, so Prime it today!)

CHAPTER FIVE

The Goal of My Spirit: Being Known by God and Others

With our tummies full, we departed from the cafeteria in song. That night would be different than other nights though, because it was the last night of camp. The whole week had been different, *very* different. SEEK camp at Lake Texoma was for kids and teens with *severe* special needs. Although I felt led to serve, my teenage brain was drained as I held the door open for the happy campers.

All of us counselors helped our kids find their seats as the guitar strummed away. "Jesus, Lover of My Soul," "Dog Breath," and "Sing and Shout" were the favorite tunes and they sang them with rigor. Their joy was amplified through the wood of the log cabin-esque sanctuary. And their joy was contagious as we were all sitting in a circle, face-to-face. It was such a worshipful hub with its roaring fire and pine beams stretching above our heads.

It had *truly* been a sacred time, one that I would never forget. After the praise set wrapped up, a few counselors and campers shared their experiences of the week and then Pastor Dennis entered the middle of the circle. He was one of the compassionate visionaries behind this camp and had such a heart for families with special needs. The spoken liturgy for Holy Communion soon filled the space, and upon the word, "wine," I noticed some movement from across the room.

STRAWBERRY WINE

Before her counselor could stop her, one of the campers had made her way down to Dennis. She had long blonde hair and did more of a waddle than an actual walk. Due to fetal alcohol syndrome, her face and body were *highly* deformed and she was the size of a seven-year-old, when she was actually eighteen. Cognitively, she was as aware and articulate as a twelve-year-old. A vivacious spirit, all 75 of us seemed to be on pins and needles to see what she was going to do next. And as Dennis turned to greet her, she confidently burst into song, "Like strawberry wine and seventeen…"

The room fell completely silent as this seemingly weak soul sang with bolstering strength. She closed her eyes and fell into the lyrics of Deanna Carter's coming-of-age, country song, "the hot July moon saw everything, my first taste of love, oh bittersweet, green on the vine, like strawberry wine."

With each note tinged with anguish *and* resiliency, soon there was not a dry eye in the house. Even Dennis teared up as he stepped back and let her have the "stage." I don't think she sang more than the chorus and a bit of a verse. Then she opened her eyes, smiled and politely wobbled to her seat, as if that was a planned part of the service. (It should have been.) Dennis thanked her and continued right on with the liturgy.

Goosebumps abounding, we all knew that we had just taken part in something out-of-this-world, something *holy*. As my ole' boss, Dave, would say, "We witnessed a thin place where heaven and earth meet." I don't take communion now without traveling back to this sacred moment in my mind.

How appropriate that a potential outcast felt so accepted to share this with us during this sacrament, a time when we are reminded of our relational covenant with God *through* our love of neighbor. While she might have been singing the song of two horny teens, what we all heard was a song of healing.

Her song took me to a place of great introspection.

What pain might have led her mom to alcoholism? Was her biological mom scared when she was pregnant? What nudge led her adoptive parents to choose her? What sacrifices were made to pay for her (many) medical bills? Is her biological mom clean now? Could her adoptive parents have ever imagined she would have grown into such a confident diva? Does she understand her biological mom's poor choices? Does she understand them enough to forgive them? Does she know what a gift she is to us counselors? Can we have extras on s'mores tonight? Can we make SEEK camp last all summer? How does she live from a place of such light, when her story started out so dark? Can I borrow some of her grit? Some of her grace? How could I see the world as she does?

I looked around the room and watched others watching her. I knew many were thinking as I was. *Ah, yes, this is you, God. Yes, this is you. Ya got our attention, and thanks for reminding us that this, this is what it's all about. This. Right. Here.*

This community had been part of her healing journey, and as she shifted my mentality, she became a part of mine.

As Rob Bell teaches on the Eucharist (communion), "The way of Jesus is the path of descent. It's about our death. It's our willingness to join the world in its suffering, it's our participation in the new humanity, it's our weakness calling out to others in their weakness. The Eucharist is what happens when the question is asked, what does it look like for us to *be* a Eucharist for these people, here and now? What does it look like for us to break ourselves open and pour ourselves out for the healing of these people in this time in this place? "[1]

3

Being hardwired for relationships, we were made to pour ourselves out for the healing of others. Not only does the Holy Spirit offer us grit and grace in the doing of life with other humans, but Godself gives us an example of this as the relational Trinity. Within the Trinity, there are three persons in one: Father, Son, Holy Spirit (or another way to look at it—Creator, Redeemer, Sustainer). While each make up the Triune God, if they were on a payroll, they would each have distinct job descriptions but would all make the same because they're all one.

Within the Trinity, we see relational energy. We see relationships.

Saint Augustine taught that it is the love that the Godhead has for the Son that not only generates the Redeemer, but out of this reciprocal love, the third member, the Holy Spirit, is born. He teaches, "Being the Spirit of the relationship between the first and second Trinitarian members, he proceeds from the [Creator] and from the [Redeemer]…The foundation for the triunity of God, therefore, lies with the eternal relationship between the Father and the Son."[2]

1   Bell; *Jesus Wants to Save Christians*, 180-181.

2   Grenz; *Theology for the Community of God*, 70-71.

Molded in the Imago Dei, the triune God desires that *all* of humanity mirror the eternal reality and essence of their Creator. God desires that we be brought into fellowship, not only for our own reconciliation, but so that we may partake in God's nature as well. (2 Peter 1:4) Since we were made for relationships, it is *impossible* to discover our true identity as beloved children of God without being part of a community. As Stanley Grenz proclaims, "Our salvation occurs in relationships, not in isolation. Hence, God's purpose includes human interaction. And it moves beyond the isolated human realm to encompass all of creation. God desires a reconciled humankind (Ephesians 2:14-19) living in the renewed creation and enjoying [God's] presence. (Revelations 21:1-5a)"[3]

Since we were designed for relationships by a highly relational Creator, some could argue that maintaining healthy relationships is the *most* important, albeit difficult, of the spiritual disciplines to practice.

Have you ever looked at it that way?

Have you ever viewed your relationships with your colleagues, friends, enemies, and that neighbor who shouldn't mow shirtless as a spiritual discipline? Yep, as part of the greatest commandment that Jesus taught (Matthew 22:36-40), this is right up there with praying, studying, fasting, and worship. As a spiritual discipline, it takes time, grace, and *lots* of grit.

LINDSAY, THE RESOLUTION

Before all the therapy and "Come-to-Jesus" moments with mentors, relationships were the one place that I didn't exude lots of grit.

---

3   Ibid., 481.

As one who used to seek out fans as opposed to friends (as undifferentiated persons often do), at the first sign of a disagreement, I would flee the relationship (be it platonic, romantic, or professional).

I'm out-of-here, Muchacho!

The majority of my friendships growing up were charity cases, in which it was my role to save them as their savior. That fact alone made me feel somewhat good about myself (a rare feeling), and since I was "saving" them, it was, as I understood it, a mutually beneficial relationship.

This way of operating might have been a survival technique during the first part of my story, as my family moved a lot, but thankfully, like all stories, a resolution finally presented itself. "Its" name was Lindsay.

We met in the elevator of the freshman girl's dorm when I was eighteen. It was move-in day. We had been informed that we were matched with each other as roommates, but we had yet to meet. She had on a pink flannel shirt, side-braid and was super-tan from life-guarding. Her smile was Julia-Roberts-big, and she strutted with the swag of a soccer-star (which she was). The admissions counselor had informed me that she and I were *perfect* for each other. When the doors parted, I had a hunch it was her and sought her consent for a hug. We both squealed with excitement, and our sixteen-year friendship commenced.

She might have thought we were just roommates who enjoyed pulling pranks on others and making a shrine for our dead fish in the hall (RIP Beast), but the truth is that she was a *major* agent for healing for me.

Through our friendship, I learned of the beauty of simply *being* without having to (always) *be* impressive. For once, I thought, "Wow, I honestly think this person would still like me even if I didn't have any talent at all." I learned that I was kind-of fun, and that I could call the shots on how much of that said "fun" I enjoyed daily. I learned that in trustworthy friendships, vulnerability is safe as opposed to weak. For the first time, I did not need to provide the strength and joy for another, for she had already obtained that for herself.

With our friendship being a beautiful balance of give and take, she not only helped me to be a better friend to *myself*, but she set the bar for *all* of my future friendships. She opened my heart to a God whose love is the furthest thing from performance-based. And above all else, she brought me closer to the healing Christ who reconciles *all* relationships and heals *all* wounds.

These relationships with self, others, and God are intertwined eternally.

And nothing more truly displays this as the symbol of my great Scottish ancestors with the Celtic Knot. "The deeper we move in our own being," unpacks J. Philip Newel, "the closer we come to Christ. And the closer we come to Christ's soul, the nearer we move to a heart of one another. In Christ, we hear not foreign sounds, but the deepest intimations of the human and the divine *intertwined.*"[4]

Now obviously, not every relationship is going to natu-rally be worth the work, but what do you gain in loving only those who love you (for even sinners do that)? (Luke 6:32) Even in (or, should I say, *especially* in) the most difficult of rela-tionships, you were made to reveal Christ to that annoying, God-forsaken-person.

It is for this reason that I believe it is pertinent to segregate the relationships in your life. Wait...that came out wrong. Let

---

4   Newel; *Christ of the Celts,* 69.

me take another swing at that. It is pertinent to slap labels on the people in your life. Is that better? No? Well, allow me to explain.

CAKE

The comedic genius, Mindy Kaling writes that instead of having *a* best friend, she has top-tier *friends*. This is superb imagery, not only because it makes me think of my most beloved food group (cake), but it implies that not all of the relationships in her life are worthy of the top-tier, but they *still* have a role to play. If there is a top-tier, there must certainly be a middle-tier, and there wouldn't be a middle-tier unless it presided over a bottom tier.

Tiers of Relationships[5]

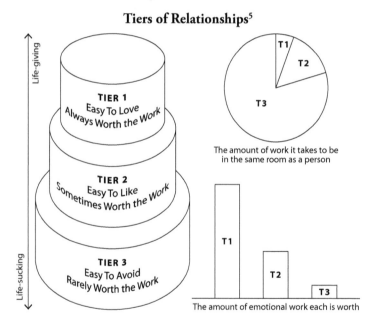

Top Tier (T1) persons are *always* worth the work, and are *easy* to love. This tier, of course, is reserved for your *most* beloved

---

5   Based off a quote by Mindy Kaling. Chart by Meggie Lee Calvin.

people in life: your significant other, your favorite child, your closest friends, and your most cherished co-worker. These relationships are the *epitome* of life-giving to you, and require very little work. If the day ever comes that work is required, these persons are worth *every* ounce of your mental, physical, and emotional energy.

Middle Tier (T2) relationships look a little different, for these persons are easy to *like* but sometimes require work. These are most often relatives who you enjoy seeing only at Christmas over a card game as to avoid talking about politics. These can also take the form of co-workers. You like these persons, and they give you a little bit of life, but at times, they flirt with being high-maintenance. If the overall health of your family or staff didn't rely on you getting along with this person, you probably wouldn't carve out time for them.

Lastly, you have your bottom-tier (T3). The stoic philosophers had a great way of describing this realm of interactions and it was with a healthy level of avoidance. Yes, these people (God bless 'em) are easy to avoid, and are *rarely* worth the work. I offer no apologies for the word 'rarely' because unless you have an undeniable divine nudge tell you otherwise, it's true.

Folks in this tier are as enjoyable as locking your keys in your car.

They are as enjoyable as putting on a long-sleeve shirt after a shower *before* you dry off.

No, wait. I've got it.

Persons in the bottom-tier are as enjoyable as finding a long, alfredo-covered hair in your *Olive Garden* pasta. (There it is.)

They personify life-suckage and are John-Denver-Rocky-Mountain-*high*-maintenance.

As life-coach, Jamal Jivanjee, shares about these types of relationships, "Everyone is infinitely worthy, but not everyone is infinitely worthy of you and your finite presence in space and time in this life."

The values of a T3 person might simply be against everything you stand for. Or on a deeper level, they might have hurt you or a loved one, so you still move with strict boundaries because you don't fully trust them.

Like the psalmist, it is best to perceive and pray from a place of authenticity instead of one of repression. It is impossible to heal muffled wounds, and often, even after we forgive someone, we find it best to keep him/her in the bottom-tier as a reminder of our boundaries. Bottom-tier folks can be the most emotionally unstable ones in our lives, and more than with the other tiers, we must remember that their emotional health is *their* responsibility—not ours. Bottom-tier relationships are simply not worth the emotional work. If you are questioning this, maybe you have incorrectly placed someone in the wrong tier.

As the tiers imply in the chart, (you're welcome) there are boundaries naturally at play here.

While bottom-tier folks will require much more rigid boundaries than top-top tier, the main boundary to honor is to simply keep people in their assigned tiers. These are not literal tiers, of course. So, what I mean by this is to uphold mental boundaries as well.

As shared on previous pages, who (or what) you allow to take up residency in your mind is *truly* all you have control over in life. So, when you are on a date with your top-tier spouse, don't be thinking about that bottom-tier dingdong from that one meeting. Put him back in his bottom-tier where he belongs. This date is so much more life-giving. This date is *so* much more important. Mr. T3 is not worth a single thought, and he's definitely not worth a conversation over mini-golf. You paid for a sitter for goodness sake! Don't waste that precious time on him! You put him back down in his bottom-tier where he belongs, and don't think about him again 'til Tuesday's meeting.

On the flip side, there are times when conversing with bottom-tier persons, that it's best to exclude your top-tier relationships all together. Oh, I don't know, say when you're listening to some highly-critical thoughts by some high-maintenance bottom-tier parents (just a little hypothetical here), your top tier relationships are *not* up for grabs. Even if they're complaining about you wearing your child while serving communion. They're not saying anything about your parenting skills, they are simply talking logistics. They are concerned about dripping juice on the baby's head. So, divorce yourself and your top-tier child from the conversation and just focus on the task at hand. Leave the top-tier relationships out of this bottom-tier conversation to assure the healthiest possible outcome.

Furthermore, there have been times that I mistakenly exerted top-tier-amounts-of-energy to mend a bottom-tier relationship, only to have the grace that I extended thrown on the ground and spat on. In retrospect, I realize it was naïve, nay, dumb, of me to expect one so emotionally immature (as most bottom-tier persons are) to know how to handle an emotionally healthy response. This was a painful realization but a necessary one. I'm slowly learning that if it's a bottom-tier relationship, I need to give it the exact amount of energy it deserves and *no* more.

Gather your gumption and maintain those mental boundaries, young grasshopper!

Obviously, persons can move tiers, but from my experience, this doesn't happen all too often. A prime example of this is Jane and Mr. Darcy in *Pride and Prejudice*. He went from a hot bottom-tier jerk to hot top-tier lover. Now, this is rare because there's only one Colin Firth and he's perfect in every way. However, as mentioned before, the opposite can also occur. Someone could hurt you and she would drop a tier or two—permanently. This too is rare though, because when a top-tier person ticks you off, the love you share for her makes it *worth* the work to preserve that status.

Only you have the power to grant folks permits in different tiers. No permission is required on behalf of anyone else. It's totally your call. As the Spirit nudges you to loosen or tighten boundaries, trust yourself to do so. As cartoonist and author, David Hayward, shares about certain folks in his bottom-tier,

"I grab a lasso [...to] face the fear of my enemy.

Why a lasso? Because I've come to believe that there are only two ways to eliminate an enemy:

Push them away. Hate them.

Bring them closer. Love them.

With the first, you must also lose yourself.

With the second, you must also love yourself."[6]

I try not to let any of my relational tiers hold space for hate, but only realistic expectations. And like humans, expectations can sometimes evolve *and* devolve.

From my experience, the quickest way persons shift tiers is if I stopped serving on a board with them. Let's say, that while on the team, I view them as a middle-tier relationship regardless if there has been some bridge burning, back-stabbing and betrayal.

---

6   Hayward, David; *The Liberation of Sophia*, 87.

My sole purpose for viewing the relationship this way is to benefit the health of the team and assist us toward our goal. Yet, as soon as I leave the team, they quickly become part of a bottom-tier relationship in my mind and are no longer worth my time or work (of any kind). They are an utter distraction from the life-giving relationships of the top-two tiers.

Yep, sometimes revealing Christ to another involves a healthy avoidance and lots of clear-cut boundaries, but at the end of the day, you can still offer them grace. So now, let's dive a little deeper into these three tiers of relationships, and to annoy you linear thinkers, we're going to go in reverse order.

BOTTOM-TIER RELATIONSHIPS: EASY TO AVOID, RARELY WORTH THE WORK.

We used to live in a house where our neighbors would rock out on their front porch with loud tunes, drinks, and illegal substances *long* into the evening. After said rocking-out, a *variety* of bodily fluids would end up in our yard. Yeah—gross. I'm all for a good time, but when you work at a church, bedtime on Saturday night is 9:30—tops. (#PartyPooperMeg) We tolerated this for five years, and were cordial, but then one Palm Sunday weekend, I had reached my boiling point and called the cops. (Please keep reading, I promise I'm not that much of a buzzkill.)

Before this story goes any further, you must know the events of the previous month.

As new parents, with one of us supervising in a start-up company, the other writing a book, both serving as full-time caretakers of our offspring, and both working well over forty-hours a week, we needed a little help with housework. After *many* tiffs between Garrett and I, he offered to get me a housecleaner and we were able to find a local undergrad who fit the bill. It was *such* a gift during a very overwhelming season, but I was *very* hesitant at first.

I felt guilty for needing help with maintaining my own home, and even more-so, I felt it made me a weaker Christian because I was not practicing good stewardship. This feels ridiculous to type, but it's true. This is exactly how I felt. This is exactly why I said "no" when he first kindly offered. This is exactly why this story is *so* worth sharing with you now, Dear Reader Friend.

Not ten minutes after I called that night, the cops arrived, and not five minutes after they drove off, I heard slurred-yelling from the mom in our front yard.

In an extremely pissed-off tone, she shouted, "Fuck you, Meg Calvin!!! Fuckin' called the cops?! Who the fuck do you think you are?! You call this being a good Christian?! You're not even a real Christian! Shit! You don't even clean your own house, you fake fucking Christian! Real Christians do their own housework! I work hard, you don't even know, you fake fucking Christian! You're such a fake fucking Christian!"

This went on for *quite* a while, until my husband bravely put on his Carhart over his jammies and joined the drunk/high mortal in our yard. And as he often does, he was able to help her find her calm.

In retrospect, this couldn't have been a more hilarious scene of her pulling on my competency *and* financial triggers. But in the moment, I was trembling in discomfort. While I was proud that, after five-plus-years, all she had on me was that I hired out some of my housework, I predominately thought that if I'm the only "real" or "fake" Christian she ever has a relationship with, I want it to at least look *somewhat* Christ-like. So, I did the only thing that I know how to do, which is to talk/write my way out of a sticky situation. At 4 a.m., after no sleep, I popped up and put on my robe.

"Where are you going?" Garrett sleepily said (because *he* fell asleep *just* fine after coming face to face with the furious, intoxicated momma).

"I've got to write her a letter," I said as I petted the nightstand for my glasses.

"Are you serious? You did nothing wrong," he said.

"I know, I know. I just can't move forward peacefully until I write to her," I said as I opened the bedroom door.

"Ok. But, no matter what, know that you were 100% justified in what you did," he replied.

"I will. I will let you read it before I run it over," I said and reported to my data fort, i.e. the kitchen table.

I wrote of how we had appreciated their patience with our noisy dog over the years, that I had a busy morning at work tomorrow, that we in no way meant for things to escalate as they did, and that we hoped that we could live peacefully as neighbors moving forward. I signed my name and dated it at the top March 21. And then at 3:30 a.m. on Palm Sunday morning, I awkwardly sprinted over in my robe and tucked the note in her mail box. Still shaking in discomfort, I finally got two hours of sleep before the big day, and we were able to live cordially in the years that followed.

This night with its abundance of comical lessons imprinted itself on my mind and early on March 22, the *following* year, the hollering momma messaged me on *Facebook* asking about our ministries at the church. I guess the memory meant something to her, too, and she finally thought I was a "real" enough of a Christian from whom her kids could learn. While our relationship would not grow beyond being cordial neighbors, I was thankful that I was able to act in a Christ-like way within a bottom-tier bond.

MIDDLE-TIER RELATIONSHIPS: EASY TO LIKE, SOMETIMES WORTH THE WORK

Not every person that is difficult to love requires a level of healthy avoidance, although it's often tempting. There are some that cross our paths personally or professionally, that our love (or at least 'like') of them is *required* for the greater good of the relational system or the company's goal. I once worked with one whose chemistry with me was as if someone lit two firecrackers and then tossed them in a sealed box. Yep—no bueno. Call it a personality clash, call it the age-card, whatever you call it, it was uncomfortable for years.

For seven years, I prayed in my journal to *authentically* love this person with the love of the Lord; not five, not six—seven. And then something incredible happened. I began to empathize with the fear that she brought to work with her each day. I began to understand her motives, and respect how she was wired differently than me. I began to take ownership of my own emotional health, so when her efficiency-valuing-self would question a dream of my innovation-valuing-self, I would not shut down emotionally, but I would simply breath deep and ask a clarifying question.

I guess you could say, that I unromantically courted her for seven years, before I was finally at a place of authentically loving her *just* as she was.

This process reminded me of my high school days when I would sing in the all-state choir. Obviously, the caliber of music was *much* more complicated, and there was one piece every year that I would loath. I would sincerely detest it at first. Thinking I would never learn it, it required *many* hours of annoyingly belting foreign languages from my loft bedroom. I kept at it though, and due to all of the focused work that I poured into the blasted thing, it would inevitably become my favorite piece.

The same exact thing happened with my co-worker. (Well, minus the foreign language part because she spoke English.) I spent *so* much time *working hard* at loving well, that after seven years, she became one of my most favorite people in the world. Because the value and intentionality in my work, I began to take great pride in our relationship as if it was a prepared Latin piece by Mozart.

Unlike my neighbor whose tie to me might have not gone any further than an apology note, ignoring the bodily fluids, and a wave as I drove to work, what developed between my coworker and I has slowly deepened in ways more glorious than I could've ever fathomed. Did we hang out outside of work? No. But as a colleague, she had my utmost respect and I truly appreciate what she adds to my life.

TOP-TIER RELATIONSHIPS: EASY TO LOVE, ALWAYS WORTH THE WORK

Some relationships take way more work than others, and *only* you get to decide which ones are worth your effort. Only you get to decide which ones call for healthy boundaries.

A bond that I believe is *always* worth working to heal and maintain is the one that I have with Dena and Mo. Whoa, that felt strange to type. I mean—my Mom and Dad.

As Stephen Covey notoriously teaches in his "little book" *Seven Habits of Highly Effective Families,* even healthy families are off-course ninety percent of the time. They are like an airplane that is only on its flight plan ten percent of the time; but the pilot has a vision for her destination and despite the external factors, continues aiming for it.

This was not always the case when I was a child. We felt like our family was only on course three-percent of the time. This is no longer true for our immediate family, but like a difficult piece of music, it has taken a great deal of intentional work and everyone in the choir doing their part to sing on key.

Through their own efforts of prayer, therapy, and spending time in God's second book, nature, my parents are finding peace with their pasts; which in turn has improved their relationships with us kids.

How healing it has been as an adult to rewrite parts of my childhood with facts. (What a novel idea!) This is possible because I've grown to understand their motives that were invisible to me when I was young. I now see that the crazy in my Mom that once annoyed in me, is the exact same crazy that protected me.

How healing it is to reflect on the darker memories of my parents, and actually see them for what they were—moments of sadness and fear; not toward *me*, but toward their own childhoods, toward their own professional grievances. I have come to believe that many emotions are too embarrassed to reveal themselves. So, they far too often disguise themselves as anger.

How healing it would've been to tell that little anxious Meg, that this too will pass. Things *will* get better. Your parents *will* get it together, and until they do, you *will* be comforted and restored by the Holy Spirit. I would've also encouraged her with the hope of the Christ-like mentors she was going to meet along the way.

I would tell that determined force of a human with brown, chili-bowl hair that these moments of fear would usher in an *abundance* of empathy and courage. And above all else, I would tell her to forgive her parents for they were just young *people* doing their absolute best with what they had (emotionally, spiritually, mentally, and physically) at the time.

I can look back now and *totally* get it. I don't justify it, nor own the blame for it, but I get it.

I totally see it more clearly; since I now see both sides, since I now know the *whole* story.

It was as if my parents had found a treasure chest but had yet to find the key, were trying to read Russian poetry before being fluent, or were mere babes as someone shoved solids down their throats. Sometimes, opportunities for us to love come *before* we are equipped to love well. Thankfully, however, there are second chances and my parents have *more* than taken advantage of those.

And forgive them I have, but this was probably easier than others because I have received sincere apologies from the both of them.

My dad has written me three apology letters over the years for his mistakes as a parent, and these have been mighty healing agents for us. My mother, to no surprise, took a much less subtle approach (very animated, she is).

I heard her sobbing from the pews as I rehearsed a song before my sister's wedding. Pulling the mic off to the side, I said, "Well, that's a good sign." *Tearful audiences are usually moved audiences, right?*

"No, no, it's not that," she said through her sniffles and sobs.

"I just don't deserve you—all of you. I have made *so* many mistakes as a parent, and I just can't believe how wonderful you've all turned out. I just don't..." she paused as she blew her woes into a tissue.

My mostly oblivious nineteen-year-old-brain was not quite sure how to respond to this, so I just hugged her and said, "You *do* deserve us, Mom, you do. And I love you." *Now, sit back down and tell me I sing pretty.* (I jest.)

As a mom myself now, who's doing a fine job of racking up mistakes with my own kid, I realize now how powerful this moment was. It took great vulnerability and strength. It took high amounts of self-awareness and (most importantly) it took a *desire* to do better as a parent, and they both did. My parents have grown *so* much over the last decade or so that I sometimes don't even recognize them. *Hey?! Who are you emotionally present conversationalists and what have you done with my parents?!*

They have put in the work, and for that, I am eternally grateful. And with a grateful heart, it's much easier to spot the light in the darkness. I can now look back and reframe some of my childhood. I can now look back and celebrate my childhood.

I appreciate that both of my parents valued surrounding us with beauty. From the yard, to our rooms, to our colorful, well-rounded meals, to camping and museum trips, beautifying our days was a *top* priority. This value is so good for the soul, and I strive to pass it on to my own offspring. While they both killed it professionally, they were both highly involved in our extracurricular lives as well. I cling to the memory of my mom helping me warm up my voice before I would take the stage, and my dad helping me to build the sweetest parade floats ever.

HOODIES AND LIPSTICK

As aforementioned, my dad's story is filled with *much* heartache, and from this high-stress space, he parented. Knowing this helps me to continually give him grace for his temper (which has greatly diminished, thank *you*, Jesus!) and it is also for this reason that the following was normal dinner conversation.

"Meg, what do you do if you are leaving the store and a man runs up to you and demands your car keys?" he says in his soldier voice, while dipping his fajita in salsa. And when I type, "soldier voice," allow me to paint you a picture, Dear Reader Friend.

My dad is an intimidating beast. He's an adrenaline junky who looks down on us weaklings who drink coffee for energy. The dude went from fighting with tanks in the Gulf War to fighting fires in the south. His ideal Sunday is listening to Maxwell on leadership while singlehandedly building a garage in a day. He towers over most people and kind-of looks like a stern Jaime Camil (the dad on the show *Jane the Virgin*). "Fun" for this guy is lassoing himself to tall trees to trim them and bouncing from cliff to cliff on his mountain bike. His best overtold story to tell is when a tree branch brutally stabbed his leg, and he got *right* back on his bike.

So, in response to this soldier, I said, "Uh, say no?" and looked to my little sister to see if she had a guess.

"Nope," he says with his disapproving head-shake, which quickly turns to a smug grin as he shares the "right" answer. "You throw your keys towards the darkest part of the parking lot, and you run towards the well-lit part of the lot. And if you ever are concerned that you can't outrun the guy, hide under a car. Just lie flat and try to be as quiet as you can. Even quiet your breathing, Meg."

"Geesh, Mo!" my mom would say from the stove as she was always the last one to eat.

Everyone would be silent from the fearful visions of this, but he was just getting warmed up.

I AM MY OWN SANCTUARY

"Ok, ok, Meg, here we go" he would say with growing excitement, as he leaned back in his chair. "If your car breaks down on the side of the road, and you can't fix that tire like I taught you, what-do-ya- do?" he asks while gesturing with his iced tea in his hand.

"Does my phone work?" I answer, already feeling stumped on second scenario of ten.

"It does, but it might take us or the cops a while to get there," he shares as he puts his tea down to fully commit to the supper sermon he is about to give.

"The cops? Why are the cops there? What's happening? Wait—did I kill a guy!?" I jokingly say, as the siblings erupt with laughter.

"Nope. It doesn't matter. All that matters is that you're going to be alone on that street for a while, so here's what you do. I'm going to put a baseball bat in your trunk and a ball cap and hooded jacket under your seat. When your car breaks down, and you can't fix the tire, you call us or the cops and then start walking. But only walk if you feel help is far away *and* carry your baseball bat. If you have to walk, you put on that hoodie and ball cap and you walk like a man on the side of the road. You just need to slouch a little bit and carry yourself like a man. The jacket and ball cap will hide the fact that you are a woman, and folks will be less likely to stop—"

"Yeah, *and* the fact that I'm walkin' down the road swinging a baseball bat like a psycho," I nervously interrupt, and the table explodes with laughter.

"No, no," he shakes his head, grins and continues. "All three are important. You need a hat, hoodie, and bat. Hopefully you won't need to use the bat, but just in case. Also, the sparkly gems hanging on your review mirror, those gotta go. Criminals stroll through parking lots looking for any car that looks feminine and then they stalk your car until you come out of the store and attack. So, your car needs to look like a man drives it."

These types of "conversations" would go on for quite a bit, and while they might have sky-rocketed my anxiety, they equipped me to move and travel with a keen eye. Seriously, wherever I am I can describe all of the people around me—their age(ish), race(ish), and clothing(ish), (along with which one looks the guiltiest). Thanks, Dad. And because I followed his advice, my travels (which became many as I aged) felt safer when I was alone in a different city.

One could say that scaring the shit out of me did wonders for my confidence and sense of awareness as an adult. All of these "drills" came from a place of protective love. Thanks to his own steps of healing that he has taken, I now observe him living from a place of being prepared for the worse, while being peacefully present in the moment. For as he and I are learning as we age, not every moment is the worse. Some people *are* actually good and worthy of your trust.

Unlike my father who only communicated through drill-like monologues, my mother was a *very* noisy creature, and her go-to catchphrases echoed through our home. She is a power-house of a woman with the energy of the *Energizer* bunny *on Red Bull.* As the writer, Michayla White, puts it, she "raised kids *and* dreams" (in the same life season) and continues to *crush* it in her career.

She looks like God mashed Jennifer Anniston and Sally Field together and then deep fat fried her in the fountain of youth. Like all true southern belles, she can be charming but can also put the "kill" in "kill 'em with kindness." She loves her four kids tenaciously and very few obtain her passion for teaching.

She is fierce, and at times unruly.

She is my mom.

Even though it is annoying when she looks at me like I don't feed my toddler or blow dry said toddler's hair, my goal has *always* been to make her laugh--to bring her joy. Her laugh is quite the experience. It is unquenchably wild, as it involves her entire body and is explosively loud. When I was in 2nd grade she and my teacher encouraged me to be a comedian, and ever since then, I have been living up to the challenge. I hope you laugh as well, Dear Reader Friend, and to enhance your experience, please read the below in a southern accent.

- Upon all four of us wanting a sip of her *Dr. Pepper* she would say with a grin, "I swear if I was drinkin' cow pee you'd all wanna drink!"

- Whenever I was experiencing friend issues at school, she would say, "Trash attracts trash, ya know? It's gonna happen naturally at work, at school, and all the days of your life. You gotta be careful with the friends you choose and maybe this friendship's not workin' out because you're not trash."

- Museum trips were huge in our family, and this was her most popular line, "Surround yourself with beauty, Meg, and you will feel better."

- While checking the bathroom of the three sisters, we would hear her shout, "There's a pink ring in this toilet!!!! Someone's gonna get a staph infection!!!"

- After a high school break up, and I was sobbing on her shoulder, she said, "One of these days, you are gonna look back and be so thankful for this moment. Even though you are crying now, *one* day you will be thankful."

- Anytime one of us was dating someone that she wished we *would* break up with she would say with a chuckle, "My prayer for you is that you land a man who does not take nearly as much work as your Dad did."

- For some reason, as I shared earlier, my mom created a new term for when she talked about physical boundaries in dating, so in my teen years I would hear, "Don't be too frothy now!" (Yes—'frothy' is the ladylike term for being too H-word.)

- After tiffs during my last year at home, she would swing open the front door and shout, "You can be mad at me, but don't you drive fast out of anger!" (I still hear this one whenever I leave a meeting angry.)

- After hours in the lake, she would holler as she picked up sopping wet swimsuits and towels, "Cootie-booty, cootie-booty, baths are not an option tonight! If ya don't bathe after playing in the lake, you *will* get cootie-booty!" ('Till this day, I'm still not sure of what medical condition she was referring to, but her strategy sure kept us all clean.)

- Church was important to my mom. I recall her leading church at our kitchen table when I was a kid because we had just moved and had yet to find a church home. One of my favorite lines regarding "the church" and its inhabitants was, "Some Saturday nights lead to you rightfully taking your place in the back pew on Sunday mornin'. That's the problem with leaders today. They don't know when to humbly step down from the front pulpit and take their place in that last pew. If your personal life is not lining up with the values of your public position of leadership, ya need to take a season of sittin' in that last pew 'til ya figure it out."

- Sometimes after a heated meeting, she will call me and say, "Ignorance, just plain ignorance. I mean--are they even thinking about what's best for the kids?!"

- Anytime I would call her to vent on a crappy day, she would end the convo with, "Tomorrow is a brand-new day. And although you can't control all of this, you *can* control how you look and feel. So wake up tomorrow and put on your lipstick and feel good about yourself!"

- (This last one needs no setup.) "My hope for all of my kids is that they speak their minds, infuse every conversation with love, know that when one door closes, the one that opens will be better, and above *all* else, I hope that they know not to fear because God *will* take care of them."

PORCH SHAMANS

While my mom would make me richer than Amy Schumer as a stand-up comedian, there is no character more unique in my top-tier than my second mom, my Aunt Nancy. As my mom's sister, she was always an integral part of our lives. And as I shared in my first book, there are times when supplemental parents are needed, and she and my grandparents filled this roll very nicely.

My Aunt wears such badges of honor as my "Cosmetic Buddha" and my "Porch Shaman." Like Moses encountering the burning bush, I feel a need to remove my shoes when I step on her porch, for it's truly holy ground. If ever God made a body too small to house the *fullness* of one's spirit, it would be that of my Aunt Nancy.

To call her stunning and wise would nearly brush the surface. She is exotically beautiful.

She is brusque. (You're gettin' your money's worth with that word, aren't ya?!)

She is intellectually brilliant and connects to nature, people and art in a way that is truly transcendental. She's a new-age poet, painter, photographer, and is unreservedly gregarious.

She has traveled to places of such darkness, only to rise above them and return with the souvenirs of hope and justice (which just happens to be the names of two of her kids). And like a true spiritual nomad, she shares these with her fellow travelers.

Many a spiritual moment took place on her porch and in her salon. As she asked deep questions, and I loved to talk, I hung out there all the time. If I wasn't just there to talk her ear off, I was there to have my hair and makeup done for some singing or speaking gig. (And we would gnaw the bone of existential mysteries while she styled.)

Our Valentine's Day mornings were spent together for years as I sang telegrams as a fundraiser. (I know. Could I've have been *any* cooler?). My Cinderella-like gown getup was made complete with a fairy-like hairdo and *way* too much glitter. No other Valentine's day will ever compete with those spent with her.

Being on the opposite end of the spectrum than my mom on *many* issues, my aunt's unfiltered ways were quite eye-opening, and implicitly led me to think for myself after weighing both of their thoughts as a teen. Even though she considered tanning by the pool while my three-year-old self swam as 'babysitting,' I really hit the jackpot with my two moms. (She was also a young teen when I was born, so I get it.)

"You just got to row your *own* boat, Meg," she would say while spraying Texas-amounts of hairspray. "For life is truly but a dream. Just keep rowing and rowing until you find the perfect stream."

And row I did.

This ability to reflect on our difficult pasts *and* see the good that God brought from *all* of it (even the scar-leaving stuff), was also inherited from the faith of my grandparents. Yep, unlike most kids that just had a parental-dyad guiding their path, I had two sets, and then a second mom as well. With my Dad being stationed away with the Army, and my mom working a lot to provide for us, my mom's parents were basically second parents versus grandparents when I was a kid.

As United Methodist missionaries, they expanded my worldview on *so* many levels. They took me to Christian conferences and retreats, encouraged me to start preaching when I was a wee lil' pup, and taught me how to roll paint and fix roofs (ok, hand them shingles) in Mexico and the Appalachians. They introduced me to healthy, faithful mentors and blessed me with professional connections that continue to carry me through life—not an overstatement.

Seriously, you won't believe this next part.

My grandparents were working with Sarah Wilke with her brand new ministry known as *Project Transformation* (*Google* it if you are an undergrad looking for a summer job.) around the time that I was 12. I joined them at a meeting once, and Sarah told me that I should go to her father's school, Southwestern College. She was right and six-years-later, I did.

Then I was hired by her sister-in-law at a church that same year. At thirty-two, I was hired by Sarah's brother at my current gig. Yep, so my entire career, in a sense, stemmed from my grandparents connecting me to a faithful community when I was young. Oh, and then to add to the fun, Lindsay (my resolution), married Sarah's nephew. (Sarah also gave me a stern talking to about not speaking or giving away copies of my book for free. So, if you got this copy for zilch, let's just keep it between you, me, and the pages.)

Get out of town, right?!

Furthermore, my grandparents convinced me at a young age that God wants *nothing more* than to heal our relationships with self and others.

They created a safe space for me to grapple with theological questions through thinkers like Joan Chittister and Thomas Merton. Even though they disagreed with some of the choices of my parents, they were always there to help to assure the best for their grandkids. And as I grew to understand the dysfunctions of our family, they would point me toward prayer and scripture to find the route for forgiveness.

The story of Joseph and his jealous brothers always spoke volumes to me. After being utterly betrayed by his brothers, Joseph was totally justified in holding a grudge or two. His brothers took him away from his Dad, sold him into slavery, and utterly robbed him of his future. Yet, as Joseph looked back over his life, he viewed it not through a vengeful lens, but one of grace. He went on not to only forgive his brothers, but also helped to care for them during a time of famine. He says in Genesis 50:20, "As for you, you meant evil against me, but God meant it for good, to bring it about that many people should be kept alive, as they are today."

Writer, Daniel Darling, shines a light on the main lesson in Joseph's highroad response, "Joseph didn't minimize the hurt against him. He pointed to his brothers and said to them, 'you meant evil against me.' We too often skip past this part and get to the good stuff: the forgiveness. Perhaps it's our desire to see resolution and reconciliation that causes us to minimize real hurts. I think we do this in our own lives as well. As Christians we are so wired for forgiveness that we forget to look at evil—evil done to us—and call it what it is." [7]

MUD WARS

My grandparents and the faithful mentors that they brought into my life, assisted me in not sugar-coating the hurt before I served up the forgiveness to my family. The more I would connect to God through prayer and worship as a teen, the louder God's voice felt in my bones—in my being. This God who heals the *nastiest* of scars, the most shattered of relationships was becoming more and more real to me. So as a preteen, I made youth group a priority.

One gathering was especially fun and formative because we had mud wars. Yep, a bunch of us sixth graders playin' around like birds in a birdbath in a disgusting pit-o-mud. It was truly sacramental, I tell you. No, no, it wasn't, but what followed was. After the mud pit, we all hosed off and made our way in to the sanctuary for worship. *Hey, the flier for this event didn't say anything about worship?! It just said "Mud Wars." I declare false advertisement, sir!*

---

7   Darling, "The Essential Art of Forgiveness in Ministry."

Following the sixteenth repeat of the chorus of "Shout to the Lord," the youth director invited us up for a time of prayer with an adult volunteer. Now, there were several youth groups there, which meant I did not know any of the volunteers upfront, but something nudged my young heart to go forward.

The music continued to play as I walked bravely down the far-right aisle. I wanted to hide my weak state, so there was no way I was joining the others in the center aisle. (Nooo, Ma'am!) There was a volunteer tucked back on the right side of the kneeling rail. (We are Methodist, so we don't call them "altars.") *Yes! She's in a perfect spot. No one will see me cry there.*

I don't remember her name, but I do recall that she was a white woman in her thirties with a denim cut-off shirt and bouncy dishwater-brown hair in a big ole' out-of-date scrunchie. She was giving off some major kind vibes, so I felt comfortable to share. When she asked how she could pray for me, I shared of my parents' separation, our recent move, and of my dad still fighting in the Bosnian conflict. I also implied some feelings of neglect from my family and how *very* lonely I felt—without appearing too weak, of course. #iGotThis

As she took my hands and prayed for me, I felt the palpable presence of the divine moving within me, and I knew that I was going to be comforted through this. Throughout my teen years, I returned to that night often; that night where I acknowledged the muddy pain that had caked up on me, so that it could be cleansed through prayer and worship.

That moment assured me that God was bringing some good out of the not-so-good parts of my family's story. And God did, but as I already addressed, my scars led to some dysfunctional relational patterns in the working world.

ALL TIER-TYPED TEAMS

It took me a while to *truly* trust my teammates. Could I trust them to keep their word? Could I trust them to still respect me if I was vulnerable? Could I trust them not to make our relationship transactional? Thankfully, I could trust the majority of my teammates with these matters. And as I discovered that I was relating to some of my teammates based off of the past choices of my family, (muchas gracias, therapist!) I became obsessed with not only healing myself, but also making the team I served *on* and the team that I served *over* (two different beasts) the healthiest they could be.

I attended any healthy team workshop I could and left no team-dynamic book unread, but the greatest lesson I found when it came to serving on a healthy team was in a "little" 1970s film called, *Monty Python and The Holy Grail.*

ROOF PYTHON

In this shared favorite of my husband and myself, this British comedy troupe of six tell the tale of a mythical, Middle Ages king who leads a band of knights on the search for the holy grail. Many don't know this, but the best actor in the bunch (their words, not mine), Graham Chapman, was an alcoholic. In fact, he was late and often clueless of his lines while shooting this ground-breaking flick.

Throughout this time, the other Pythons patiently loved him through it and helped him reach his potential as an actor. They believed in him, not only as an actor but as a person. Because of his talent and dedication, it was worth the work (more on this later) to keep him as a valuable teammate. They continued to believe in him and their love paid off as Chapman went on to star as the lead in their next film *The Life of Brian* and *totally* crushed it.

Sometimes, in order to be a healthy team, we have to fling another's arm around our neck and lovingly carry him towards the best version of himself (personally and professionally). Most of the time, this takes more than just one person. It requires a team doing *whatever* it takes to help another get to where God wants him to be.

I cannot watch *The Holy Grail* (which we do often) without thinking of the friends who wouldn't stop at anything to get their hurt friend to Jesus in Luke 5:17-20.

"One day, while he was teaching, Pharisees and teachers of the law were sitting nearby (they had come from every village of Galilee and Judea and from Jerusalem); and the power of the Lord was with him to heal. Just then some men came, carrying a paralyzed man on a bed. They were trying to bring him in and lay him before Jesus; but finding no way to bring him in because of the crowd, they went up on the roof and let him down with his bed through the tiles into the middle of the crowd in front of Jesus. When he saw *their* faith, he said, "Friend, your sins are forgiven.""

Like the five pythons (who would potentially be offended that I am using them to illustrate a Biblical truth after so many Christians treated them so poorly after they released their hilarious second film) carried Graham when he was struggling, the pals of this paralytic did the same. They approached the house where they had heard that Jesus would be only to see that Jesus' publicist had done a heck of a job and his popularity had grown.

The place was so packed that they couldn't get in. So what did they do? They did what any of us would do in that situation, (not!) and made their own door—through the roof.

Nothing could stand in that team's way of accomplishing their goal of getting their fellow "teammate" to Jesus.

Wouldn't it be great if on your next staff retreat, instead of doing high-ropes together, you simply reenacted this scripture? I mean, it's basically the first high-ropes exercise ever, right? It's just jam-packed with lessons on teammates—communication, trust, creativity, risk-taking, delegation, resourcefulness, etc.

And to add to the beauty of this moment, Jesus affirms the friends (teammates) as agents in their friend's salvation when he uses the phrase, "When he saw *their* faith." There is no doubt that this was a team effort. If it were not for the friends (teammates) working together so beautifully, this friend wouldn't have found healing and wholeness in Christ.

When serving on a team, sometimes you carry your teammate toward the person God intended him to be and collectively stop at nothing until that goal is accomplished. But what does it look like when you are the boss?

HUMANBOSS

This section of the book could have been titled "girlBoss," but I honestly am not a fan of this trend. Don't get me wrong, I am a feminist and am *all* for being judged by my abilities and not my anatomy, but "girlBoss" has never sat well with me.

I prefer not to put people in boxes based on their gender. Although I acknowledge that our brains and bodies are designed differently, this in no way means that all of my male teammates will be motivated the same way or vice versa for the non-male-type. Plus, despite many of the negative narratives of my childhood, my parents and grandparents never placed any restrictions on me professionally because I was a female, especially in roles of leadership. Because of this, I'd much rather just be "The Boss" (or "humanBoss") instead of "girlBoss."

I realize though in typing this that my supportive career path on a church's payroll is rare. Not once was I ever made to feel substandard by my male coworkers or bosses—not once. I was entrusted with just as much responsibility and received equal wages. I asked for my first raise as a twenty-three-year-old and it was granted. I have led over teams of both genders, and authentically connected with each person.

I detest the fact that this is not the case for all women, and I realize that my perspective may read as the exception, but it's mine and as Jo March teaches in *Little Women*, "you must write what you know," and *this* is what I know. (#ImaJoAndaMeg) I prefer to write about leadership in a way that is applicable *regardless* of gender. (What a concept?!)

And why do I think this is possible, you ask? Well, as I continue beating this dead horse, *every* personality test that I've ever taken describes me with what we in the west would consider 'masculine' terms. So, to you my Dear *Male* Reader Friend, apparently, I get you. Yep, I might do my hair and make-up *each* day like it's the talent portion, but apparently my innards are all male? I have the energy of a positive wrecking ball, I compartmentalize mentally, I move swiftly, I prefer to fire *then* aim, and when my work hat is on, I sadly often put the "product" before the "person."

When I was in the process of ordination back in 2006, the psychologist literally said to me (during the required psych evaluation), "You have what we call in this field, a very masculine leadership style." *What the what?! What does that even mean, man?*

One tool that enabled me to embrace my temperament is Carol Tuttle's work in *Living Your Truth*. We touched on this earlier, and I would like to unpack it a little further now. With Carol's help, you can dress your truth, parent through your truth, and even decorate out of your truth. (You *can* handle the truth, man.)

I discovered her work while at an Enneagram retreat, and as a female who was often told as a child to "slow down," "be still," and "stop making drama," it was very assuring. Those like me are in *no way* dainty but live for the rush of a risk, the chase of a goal. At any age, if we don't have an adrenaline high planned through a deadline or an incident (performance or athletic event) of sorts, we create one through an outlet that is often unhealthy, especially in our younger years. Those who share my determined nature live to propel ourselves and others toward action, and I guess by American standards, this sometimes makes me less feminine??? Really?!

Does it?

No way, right?

What do these human-made labels even mean? Can anything be gleaned from them?

Very possibly, for as life coach, Jamal Jivanjee shared with me on the phone, "Within me resides both the masculine and feminine energies and both are necessary." One shouldn't be looked down on when he/she expresses himself/herself in a way that is opposite from his/her gender for the interconnectedness of both expressions are needed.

Jamal went on, "In God, we see the fullness of both genders. God is gender-full, and the beauty of these different expressions can be observed all throughout our natural world. All of creation is a manifestation of how these energies work together. Each human reflects this reality about the divine as well. Within each person is both masculine and feminine energies. Yes, in a normative way, even though we have a combination of both the feminine and masculine energies within ourselves, we express predominantly through the lens of our genders [which would *totally* justify the #GirlBoss movement]—but a healthy balance of each of these energies within each of us is needed."

The famous cartoonist and author, David Hayward (The Naked Pastor), unpacks this even further with, "Some psychologists suggest that a man will discover in the woman he is attracted to the reflection of his anima, his inner female. The mysterious and beautiful feminine that he is blind to in himself he adores in the woman in front of him."[8]

I would agree with Sir Naked on this one, for the opposite was most certainly true when I fell for Garrett. The gentler way he lived from his masculine energy was *so* foreign to me. I couldn't get enough of it! I now realize that this is because within him is a healthy intermingling of both the masculine and feminine energies. I would imagine this would be the case for any emotionally stable person, yeah?

And, maybe, just maybe, because I was so comfortable in living out of both of these energies, he felt confident to keep doing the same, and yadda, yadda, yadda, we were engaged eight months later.

He lives from a place of *highly* sensitive intuition, and is reserved and moves subtly. As typed before, if I bring the force of a Niagara Falls into a room, he brings that of a calming weeping willow. He probably gets way more cuddle hours in with our toddler because I would much rather be at the park with her. He is content to just sit and talk with her—or just "be" with

---

8   Harward, David; *The Liberation of Sophia.*

her. Thanks to our flattering energy types, she might only need a little therapy as she ages.

Our temperaments do flatter each other, and whenever either of us leads from a place that is opposite of our gender, it is valued and appreciated.

I will never forget when we were watching the film *A Knight's Tale* together. This is the tale of a knight, William Thatcher (Heath Ledger) who rose above his unfortunate life factors and became a champion medieval jouster. While it was already one of Garrett's faves, I was really only watching it because Tuttle's guidance suggested that this film would align perfectly with my nature. (I go *all* in on my self-help adventures)

All throughout the flick, I was (annoyingly) commenting on how I did not relate to *any* of the female characters, and I did not understand why my girl, Carol, would suggest such a film. *Does she not know me as well as I thought she did?*

He jokingly rolled his eyes, smiled, and sincerely gave me the greatest compliment *ever*, "Don't you get it? *You* are William Thatcher." (Mic. Drop.)

He's always making me feel all warm and fuzzy and affirmed, and it might explain why he loves such warm-fuzzy-feel-good shows like *Friends* and *The Andy Griffith Show*. Some in the US might consider this 'feminine', but he (unlike me) does not hold back tears when he is touched by something of beauty and depth.

How touching, yeah?

Taking risks is not his thing—at all. Opposite of me, he believes that a plan should *not* be pursued until he has had an *ample* amount of time to think through his *perfect* plan to assure no mistakes. In fact, when he became part of his highly success-ful start-up company, he told me after he accepted the position, that if it wasn't for my advice, he would've never taken the gig because of the high-risk factor.

Needless to say, you want to get my attention? Start with challenging me.

You want to get his attention? Start with making him feel comfortable.

It is this reason that marrying him enhanced my *personal* life, as I need assistance in feeling comfortable in my desire for comfort. In marrying me, I enhanced his *professional* life, as he needs help in working through the discomfort that comes with (necessary) work-related risks.

I have been so thankful for the works of Jamal Jivanjee and others who have helped me to recognize and celebrate the coexistence of *both* the feminine and masculine energies within everyone. But this breakthrough has left me more and more annoyed when folks are judged by their anatomy and not their abilities.

This stance sometimes gets me labeled as a male chauvinist.

Allow me to explain. In the midst of digging through speaker applications for a conference, there was one applicant who labeled her talk, "How to Lead Men."

Ooooh, you bet your bottom dollar I was triggered!

Who was this woman that claimed to know *all* men everywhere? And if my husband and I don't match the western masculine and feminine stereotypes, there most certainly are others.

What an unhealthy assumption to judge all of your unique teammates by their anatomy; to simplify the calling of a servant leader to a forty-five-minute-workshop with four little steps on 'men.' Sessions like this do nothing but extend the shelf life of our gender wars by relishing on our differences, as opposed to coming together through our similarities.

Ridiculous! (I'd better start some deep breathing, or there's going to be another side sermon!)

SIDE SERMON #3?

We want to empower women to lead?

Unless a workshop is going to encourage them in better understanding themselves so that they may better understand and motivate those they serve as distinct and valuable individuals, (More to come on this in a bit.) I'm not interested!

Needless to say, I was *so* disturbed by the mere idea of this workshop submission that I gave it the lowest rating possible.

I was sharing this with Garrett when he laughingly said, "Ya know the board is going to be scrolling through the results and when they get to yours, they're gonna think, "Jeez! Who's this male chauvinist who is hating on women in leadership?"

To which I proudly protested with a chuckle, "If me wanting leaders of all genders to judge their teammates on their ability and *not* on their anatomy makes me a male chauvinist, then so be it. There is *no way* in heck I'm going to support a closed-minded workshop like this. This workshop is offensive to men to put them all in the same box, and offensive to women to assume that leading men is their problem that needs solving."

My nickname of male chauvinist stuck around for a bit.

I know, I know...this is not the case for all females in leadership, but as I shared a few lines back, I can only write what I know, while at the same time my heart breaks for female leaders whose story reads differently. So, whether you identify as a "girlBoss" or "boyBoss" or just "The Boss", I would love to give you a gift.

After ten years of building teams in the nonprofit world, I have gathered (and summarized) my top ten tips for nurturing and refining healthy volunteer teams, and for no extra cost, these are yours for the taking. Enjoy, Dear Reader Friend. (You thought all you paid for was a book, but you thought wrong!)

BABY DOLLS & LEGOS: LESSONS FROM A TODDLER'S PLAYROOM ON NURTURING & REFINING VOLUNTEER TEAMS

While I was not serving at the church, I was most likely in my daughter's playroom. As an imaginative two-year-old, she adored baby dolls and Legos. She loved wrapping the doll in blankets, patting her back, and feeding her broccoli and tuna in a highchair. I joined her and do all that I could to assure the utmost comfort for the little one. This is quite difficult because she was just fed broccoli and *tuna*.

After a while of this, the attention shifts to Legos. Her standards of a successful Lego session were, "Taller! Taller! Taller!" Once the structure was complete, my role was to assess the "building" for its stability. With her permission, (of course) I would spot the unbalanced/out of line sides and add or take away blocks. I knew my work was done when the head contractor said, "Good Job, Ma!" and applied force to check my work.

While juvenile, both of these contain helpful lessons on volunteer team leadership and man, do we ever need help! Too bad my daughter's not a toy soldier fan because there are occasions in the trenches of ministry where that is a much more fitting metaphor. Propelling a team towards progress sometimes feels like a battlefield; what with its miscommunications, personality clashes, misplaced priorities, and a lack of self-management skills within the squadron.

I could see why some want to give up on the dream of a healthy team. They want to give up on the relational covenant (1 Corinthians 12:14) to which they have been called. They think their attempts at empathy, prayer, and reading team dynamic books have *all* been in vain; and they resolve to simply show up for the remainder of their term. They stop striving for an 'A.' They settle for an average grade in the course.

But then I am reminded that Christ did not give up on us nor does he ever. It is for this reason that we should not give up on each other. We need each other. It is *only* in Christian community that we discover our true identity (1 John 4:12). In order to become who God created us to be, we cannot go at it alone. More importantly, our broken world *desperately* needs strong ministerial teams (Matthew 5:14-16). (Can I get an Amen?!)

After years of searching (accompanied by the occasional day of crying and cursing) for the secrets to nurturing and refining a strong, Spirit-led volunteer team, I have come to the conclusion that I have most likely made it more difficult than is necessary. Could the route to a healthy volunteer team be as simple as intuitively nurturing your teammates (as one does with a baby doll) while *also* maintaining a critical, keen eye (as one does with Legos) as the "structure" of the team develops?

THE BABY DOLL APPROACH: INTUITIVELY NURTURING

Decide to Listen. This may occasionally mean a late-night text with a prayer concern or a spontaneous chat at your office. Come out from behind your computer and be fully present with them in the conversation. If this calls for hot tea, an impromptu prayer, or a church-appropriate-off-to-the-side hug you don't want to miss these cues. BE FULLY PRESENT WITH THEM! :) Good listening can create holy ground.

James Sullivan teaches in the Pastoral care book, *The Good Listener*, "When you give me your full attention, as though I am the only person in the world at the moment, I feel wrapped in warmth and care. You have taken the trouble to enter into my world and to see things from my point of view. I feel understood. I feel cared for."[9] He goes on to teach that, "Good listening is such an act of loving that we can even substitute it for the word "love.""[10]

Sullivan also teaches the four Steps of Listening

- **Step out of my own world:** I must set aside my own preconceived notions and preferences before a conversation. Consider it a form of dying to oneself.

- **Enter into your world:** Empathize with them, aim to see the world through their eyes.

- **Sensing deepest feelings:** Not as important as the top two, but as I listen to you share, I am going to be seeking the underlying issue. What is the real problem/fear at play here? I will seek for this by watching your body language, facial cues, hearing different inflexions in your voice, and listening for any recurring words, persons, or themes as you share.

---

9   Sullivan, *The Good Listener;* 33.

10   Ibid., 97.

- **Giving an adequate response:** This is essential. I need to let the person know I understand them so he is not left in an awful quandary. My silence at the end can make him feel as though I am blaming or judging him. This need not be a long, eloquent speech, but something more effective. It can be as simple as, "Wow, that's really tough." Or "Gee, I am awfully sorry." It can even be no words but a pained look in the eyes while you give them a hug. The main thing is to show them that I understand them, I feel badly for them and I care. That's it.

Obey Their Gifts, Personalities, & Limitations. While it would be ideal if all of your teammates were emotionally healthy/self-aware people, this is not always the case. Some of your teammates might be completely oblivious to their limitations/vices, and God can use you to lovingly guide them towards this awareness (more to come on this in the Lego approach). As one who believes in the priesthood of all believers (1 Peter 2:5) and the different talents with which we have all been blessed (Romans 12:6-8), a big part of your role is to empower your teammates to discover these. One personality assessment that was truly helpful for our team was the Servant By Design/Process Communication Model option.

All this is to say, if a volunteer on your team fails, and you did not do everything in your power to set them up for success by honoring *all* of the above, you are partially to blame. #hardtruth

Let Them Like Their Job. Go the extra mile and give them a partner with whom they have good working chemistry. Grant them their preferred days and times to serve. Offer them as little or as much say in their area of leadership as they so desire. A Stanford study reads that the top three reasons folks don't volunteer are: they are too busy and volunteer schedules are inflexible, the job descriptions are unclear and not interesting, and (simply put) no one asked them to serve.[11]

Learn Their Drink Order. This seems menial, but this small gesture shows they are more than a "bucket-o-talent" to you. They are people with preferences, and you care about those preferences. In this line of work, we are called to wear both the ministerial and managerial hats. Simple gestures like this help greatly with the first hat.

Strengthen Conversations. These will not only enhance your professional bond with them as valued teammates, but it will also enhance the overall ministry because you are allowing the Holy Spirit to guide the conversation. These questions can be as simple as, "What has God revealed to you about yourself this semester of serving? Are there any talents/gifts from which you enjoy serving that are not being utilized? What parts of your position bring you the most joy? What supportive steps can I take to make this a more enjoyable role for you?" Volunteers are (most likely) over-committed people. If they pressed pause on their lives to meet with you over a latte, make it worth their while.

Sullivan teaches that there are three main types of communication.[12] Know what you are going for before the conversation with a volunteer begins.

---

11   Amy Yotopoulos. "Three Reasons Why People Don't Volunteer and What Can be Done About It." *The Sightlines Project.* http://longevity. stanford.edu/three-reasons-why-people-dont-volunteer-and-what-can-be-done-about-it/.

12   Sullivan, *The Good Listener;* 111.

Advice: This is *requested* guidance that I need from you about an area of knowledge where you have greater learning and experience. When I seek this from you, I do not resent you telling me what to do. The advisor must stay on topic and not try to speak to issues that he/she is not an expert in, and the advisee must feel free to alter or disregard this advice since at the end of the day-that's all it is.

Persuasion: This is an effort on my part to get you to agree with my ideas or with my plan of action. This type of communication is mainly action oriented. As the persuader, I present the goal clearly, and offer the best reasons as to why I think you might find this idea/goal attractive as well. The persuader does not impinge upon the other's freedom and listens well as the persuadee ask questions, disagrees and speaks to the loss he/she might experience if he/she does come on board with the idea. *This is not manipulation!* The goal of persuasion is agreement and truth.

Self-revelation: The most important type of communication. This is about feelings. The goal is not agreement, but understanding, acceptance, and care. The listener does not have to agree in order to understand or affirm my feelings. The big mistake that is made in this type of conversation, is when the listener confuses it for a persuasive conversation. In a conversation that is based on self-revelation, the goal is not to change anyone's ideas or course of action. It is simply to affirm one's feelings.

THE LEGO APPROACH:
STRATEGIZING KEENLY & CRITICALLY

Now before you go running for the hills with discomfort, hang with me. The Lego approach will be much easier if it is preceded by the baby doll approach. They work interchangeably, but the baby doll approach should be the foundation to create a healthy team dynamic.

Liabilities come when vices outweigh talents. This is a liability to your team and the reputation of your program. A high maintenance teammate can be a huge distraction from the ministry to which God is calling you. Plus, your other teammates will suffer if the majority of your attention is used on damage control for this one volunteer. After the second or third apology to parents, you might need to ask yourself, "Is this simply a rough edge of this volunteer who is serving out of her gifts and has loads of potential?" or "Is this is a red flag that this teammate is either A) not emotionally/spiritually healthy at the moment to fulfill this role or B) not serving out of her gifts?" Either case calls for an honest conversation. The latter calls for a potential break from serving or some grace-filled redirection towards a different position.

The creator of SNL, Lorne Michaels, when asked about the forty-plus-year success of the show, said that his secret (which his mentee/friend, Tina Fey has adopted on her shows) is to assure the "crazy" (which is common in comedians) does not outweigh the talent. This is an all-too-common concern among comedians since they don't have a track record of being the most emotionally healthy. He says as he looks back over his many years of work, the biggest issues have occurred when the "crazy" outweighed the talent. (More to come on this one!)

Express Strategically. Varying levels of personalities, life stages, and situations call for different types of communication outlets. Keenly discern the best one. Does the topic at hand call for a text, *Google Hangout,* email, phone call, face to face in your office, or a walk around the park? Each of these has their perks and drawbacks, and choosing correctly will prevent fall out from potentially sensitive subjects. 'Typing' from experience, many a bad day will be prevented if the right communication route is chosen. My rule of thumb: when in doubt, face-2-face it out! With 93% of communication being nonverbal, there are times that you are going to need to be able to read facial expressions, body lingo, and even silences to assure an effective conversation.

Give 'em time. ("No" now does not mean "No" forever.) Think critically of the ideal timing of recruiting based on a person's life. If the Holy Spirit has led you to call this person, don't give up on him/her. Now, this is *not* synonymous to pestering. If seamstress Sandy says sewing (complementary tongue twister) for the Christmas play is too much with her teaching schedule, then make a note in your calendar to call her in June for the VBS costumes. I never recruited CPAs to volunteer during tax season, and I never recruited fair workers in July. You know as well as I that their hearts are hungry to serve, they are simply awaiting direction *at the right time!*

Observe Your Boundaries. This can mean different things. To me, it means that I do not talk about volunteer needs when I am off-the-clock *unless* the person brings it up to me first. I don't want others to run away when they see me in the bread aisle for fear I might hound them for their time or talent. I also keep healthy boundaries by *only* speaking on issues that I am "over" (#busychurch) and delegating the rest to the right personnel. This naturally builds up the rest of our team and eliminates some potential miscommunications.

Brené Brown teaches in the book, *The Gift of Imperfection,* that it is much easier to have compassion towards others once you have established clear boundaries with them. Boundaries are key when seeking a sustainable serve, not only boundaries with people but with technology as well.

Ruby Wax teaches that in order for stress not to wipe us all out by 2020, we must learn to navigate technology. One way to do this is to intentionally adjust your notifications on your phone/computer. Use Google voice.

A New York Times article teaches that it takes the brain 25 minutes to regain focus on the task at hand after checking an email.[13] Yikes! One tool to help with this is to simply pause your Gmail. This chrome extension rocks!!!

All in all, when it comes to boundaries, be okay with turning your phone off, teach your team *explicitly* the best way/time to reach you, and of course, aim to play and rest a little harder than you work!

Speak to Pain While you "cannot fix [the teammates described above], it is your job to control them and in some cases, protect others on your team from them" teaches Todd Whittaker. In his fantastic book, *Shifting the Monkey; The Art of Protecting Good People from Liars, Criers, and other Slackers,* he equips you to handle the most difficult personalities on your team in a strategic (non-manipulative) kind of fashion. I seriously cannot brag enough about this book! It truly is a mind-blowing and ministry-enhancing experience.

---

13   Bob Sullivan and Hugh Thompson. "Brain Interrupted" *New York Times.* (2013 May): https://www.nytimes.com/2013/05/05/opinion/sunday/a-focus-on-distraction.html.

Todd shares, "Don't you hate it when certain teammates get away with shirking their responsibilities, while those that are already overworking pick up their slack and there is no accountability? Don't you hate it when negative, poorly performing people tend to get a disproportionate amount of power, attention, and empathy? Whittaker argues that they continue to behave obnoxiously and unfairly because they're rewarded for doing so."[14]

To stop the above issues, he suggests that in any team meeting, ask yourself these 3 questions:

- Where is the monkey (the shouldered responsibility/obligations)?

- Where should the monkey be?

- How do I shift the monkey to its proper place?

Then to get the monkey to the proper teammate, he suggests,

- Treat everyone well.

- Make decisions based on your best people. If not, your best teammates will get so uncomfortable by the culture of your team (that was randomly created by your weakest teammates} and leave or simply stop being one of the best out of spite.

- Protect your good people (responsible, faithful, well-intended teammates) first.

One simple way that I applied Todd's guidance for dealing with a slacker on my volunteer team occurred during the usual

---

14   Whitaker, *Shifting the Monkey;* 4.

rush of a Sunday morning. As I was setting up for children's worship after Sunday school, a volunteer approached me.

"You need to email all 2nd grade parents and remind them when Sunday School is out so I don't have to wait with kids," she said.

My heart rate increased; I immediately began typing the email in my head. But then I stopped and thought, *Wait a minute?! This is not my monkey, but hers. This is her classroom. She was trained to ask parents at drop off if the kids were to walk to their parent's room or wait for them to come back and get them.* Then I physically felt the monkey that she had placed on my back being moved off of me.

I confidently asked, "What kids were you waiting with?"

"Oh," she said in a calmer tone. "It was only one kid—just one family, the Winklevoss's."

"I see," I responded. "What did the Winklevoss's say when you asked them about pick up time?" (Me asking this question in a kind, non-manipulative way, held her accountable to a high standard.)

"Well," she explained, "I'm so sorry, I forgot to ask them. Don't worry about emailing all of the parents, I will just be clearer with the Winkelvoss's next week."

"Splendid!" I said. "Thank you so much for all of your work!"

The whole book is full of equipping conversational guides like these that will help you take your team's serve from good to great.

Bottom line: If you lead a team of humans, and wish to manage all of your relational tiers well, this book needs to be a yearly read of yours, Dear Reader Friend. Now enough about work, let's settle down and talk about marriage.

HOY CELEBRAMOS EL AMOR

(Today, We Celebrate Love.)

(Part of the vow renewal ceremony for my grandparents that I was privileged to officiate—in Spanish, because my Dad thinks he is funny.)

Today calls for much celebration.

Today we celebrate the growth of this couple as individuals and we celebrate all that exists because they joined their lives many years ago.

And even though some parts of the journey were not easy to love, today we celebrate love.

Similar to pilots having an intended flight path, yet despite their best efforts, they are only on track 10% of the flight due to environmental factors; there are times in marriage when we don't feel like we are on track—on track with ourselves or with our partner.

But like the pilot, who is consistently trying to get back on track, and who usually lands a successful flight, the best of partners constantly aim for the best version of their marriage and hold the other accountable to the best versions of themselves.

When one partner veers away from her strength and is operating out of fear, the other helps her to get back on track.

When one's line of sight is blocked by foggy sadness, the other cleans the windshield with a hopeful perspective.

When one partner took a wrong turn out of confusion, the other tosses him a compass of clarity.

And when one partner thinks all is lost, and that they will never find their destination, it is only found in working together.

This type of loving commitment does not just benefit the couple, but others as well, for out of their love will flow a Christ-like love onto others.

As it teaches in 1 John 4:12, "No one has ever seen God, but if we love one another, God lives in us and God's love is made perfect through us."

Working hard at loving well is *always* worth it because it is through these efforts that we experience true life with God.

SAVING THE BEST FOR LAST

"You met because your solitudes border each other's. You have shared interests and convictions. The healing paths you have chosen to travel are parallel. Along with fertile borders of your solitude where your lives meet, plant a garden together, a sacred garden. Sow the seeds of kindness and tenderness and truth there. Cultivate the garden of shared interests and concerns, of common challenges and treasured friends." (Patricia Lynn Reilly)

As displayed in the chart, top tier relationships are not only for our spouses or lovers, but I would like to take the next few paragraphs to celebrate mi esposo because he has helped me greatly at feeling safe and loved within my own sanctuary.

GARRETT, MY GARRET

I most likely will never doubt the existence of God because of the leading of this word nerd to a husband named *Garrett*. Now if that's not divine intervention, I don't know what is.

Allow me to explain.

A garret is often romantically associated with starving artists and creatives. They would return to these high, attic-like nooks above the rest of the world to find their calm and inspiration for their work. A garret was a Creative's retreat. Before that, its origins were French based on the word "guerite," which meant a watchtower of a soldier standing guard.

Garret—a creative's retreat where one finds protection, peace, and creative mojo.

No better word describes what my husband is to me than his own name. Garrett is *my garret.*

How fun is that?!

While I do not need a Fitbit to tell me this, it is so amazing to watch my heart-rate decrease as soon as he enters a room. His presence brings me immediate peace. As has been made very clear through these pages, I don't need any help in the "self-motivation" department; *however,* I do need loads of help in the relaxation department. His uncanny ability to make me LOL my work-related stress away is a true gift.

Not only is he the garret to this Creative, but we are also *often* compared to Leslie Knope and Ron Swanson (as shared before) from the NBC show *Parks and Rec.* Yep, if Ben Wyatt would have never been in the picture, and Leslie and Ron would have connected romantically, *this* would be Garrett and I. To. A. T. It's as if the genius creators of that show secretly documented both of our lives as the basis for these characters. Just like this dynamic duo, we are equal partners, whose skill sets complement each other and we always have the other's back.

There have been (thankfully only) two *very* tense meetings that I had to attend over these many years in the church. At both of them, without me even asking, Garrett joined me as my support system. (Let it be known that these were meetings where others were invited.) In these moments where I felt utterly defeated, he just held my hand under the table, silently reminding me that I could and *would* rise above.

In the same way, I have nurtured and protected him during moments of potential anxiety and discomfort because that's what partners do.

One is not the alpha and the other, the beta, because we are not a pack of dogs.

We are equally intelligent, talented, and wise humans who are *ridiculously* obsessed with the well-being (in and *outside* of the home) of the other. One does not lack for anything without the other, but life sure is *a lot* more fun and hope-filled with the other. From this space of joyful, all-consuming love, we know when to trust the other's lead, and when to *both* work towards a compromise in a decision. We *both* provide for and protect our family. We *both* nurture our family, and we *both* build a nest for our family.

I once heard a weak joke by a comedian that women will get equal pay when they are the first to run downstairs when an intruder breaks in (instead of their husbands). I am proud to say that in the one scare we had, Garrett and I both walked toward the disturbance *together*. This might also have something to do with the fact that we met on a sparring mat in a martial arts class, but that's neither here nor there. (Take that Mr. Standup with your lame joke!)

Though our wirings complement each other, we are *equally* moving through life together encouraging the other to gather his grit and forge onward toward the person (personally and professionally) that God made him to be.

It's comical how many divorced couples say things like, "We had to end our marriage because we were no longer the people that we were when we got married." Well-boy-howdy, one would *hope* that at age forty-six you weren't the same person you were at twenty-two. I don't know about you, but I was the most narcissistic, selfish, two-faced, immature, flaky person ever when I was twenty-two. I wouldn't want to be married to me either. Thank goodness God is not done with me yet, and I am still maturing.

But that's not the goal, is it? For each person to remain unchanged from the day they slipped on that ring? No way!

The goal is to evolve together. The goal is to help mend each other's wounds from the first chapters of life. The goal is to help the other polish away his areas of growth and live in a way that honors his gifts. So, I guess, when you marry someone, you are selecting a partner (in a sense) based on his/her past, present and potential. It's as if on your wedding day you are looking at all of the lovely pieces of the Ikea piece you just bought, and over the next (hopefully) sixty-five years, you will see the grey, overpriced, hutch take shape and fulfill its purpose.

You say, "I do," to *all* of the pieces of your partner; to his past (and by this, one could infer his nuclear family/roots), his present (personality and quirks), *and* his potential (hopes, dreams, goals).

Or, you could just marry for looks and hope for the best. I mean, there is no better coping mechanism than a good-looking person to lean on for support, right? I jest (kind of).

Regardless if it was the loss of a loved one, failed adoption, or a high-risk pregnancy, Garrett always succeeds at comforting me with humor. He truly is my live-in comedian. Seriously—so flippin' funny.

PEPPA PIG AND A RACIST

I often think we could follow the example of Jim and Jeannie Gaffigan and co-write humorous pieces together. Unlike me, though, Garrett has the gift of brevity. (As she types in a 63,000-word-book.) And with that, here are some of his best comedic bits.

One day while watching the poorly animated, yet strangely enduring show, *Peppa Pig,* with our daughter, he just shook his head and said, "And this is why they [the Brits] lost the war."

Then there was the time that we met the parents of our daughter's new friend.

Henley had been at pre-school for two months, and she had endlessly talked about a new friend she had made. While at a concert, I spotted her parents, and suggested to Garrett that we go and introduce ourselves.

After the formalities of handshakes and small-talk, I did my extrovert duty and wrapped up the convo in saying, "Well, I guess it's good to see that we're all normal. You always hope when your kid befriends someone that the kid's parents aren't a couple of whack-jobs, right?" Everyone awkwardly laughed, and we went our separate ways.

While we were walking away, Garrett chuckled and said, "Really? You just had to say that last part there, didn't ya?"

I sassily snapped my head back at him with a grin and said, "What? Ya know they were thinking it. Every parent thinks that. I was just acknowledging it. We are normal, and it seems they are too. So there."

We got back to our seats, and he said, through his laughter, "Yes, but it's all about *how* you put words to what people are feeling. There's a big difference between saying 'Have a nice day!' and 'Enjoy the next 24 hours.'"

And finally, although I could go on and on with the moments of nearly pee-your-pants-laughter that he has brought into my life, I present to you the time we went on a double-date.

We were at a hipster-like, farm-to-table joint with a couple who, for some reason, I was working *way* too hard to impress. They were sexy elitists and were *beyond* academically awe-inspiring.

During drinks, the wife *implied* that she thought that everyone who wore camo was racist. While I greatly disagreed with her, I sheepishly did not refute her joke because I'm a prideful person who needs lots of mental help. It was at this moment, Dear Reader Friend, that my reserved husband decided that this, of *all* double dates, would be the time that he became *passionately* long-winded.

He not only called her out on her implicit bias, but he humorously vowed to wear his camo hat on every double-date, thereafter, to expand her mind that not all camo-wearers were racists, and that is exactly what he did. He would sometime even comically wear a camo shirt. The four of us became good friends, and I stopped working hard to impress them years ago.

Together, Garrett and I seek to find light and laughter in even the most annoying of moments, and our first date after becoming parents was no different.

We were both ecstatic, for it had been a while since we had gone out *alone*, and we couldn't get our tiny human to the sitter's house fast enough. As we merged on to the bypass, we heard the most horrifying sound that anyone behind the wheel could hear—that disgusting, back-of-the-throat sound that preludes vomit. Before I could turn around to help, she had exploded. It was *everywhere.* It was on her, on me, on the car—everywhere.

We called the sitter and said we still wanted to go on a date, for she was just car sick, but that we would rush home to change (everyone) first. When we got home, we realized that we had locked the keys inside of the house, and our spare key was at his mom's house which was twenty-minutes away. As we were driving to get the key with our oddly happy, stinky baby, I propped my feet up on the dash, leaned my seat back and began to sing along with the radio.

He turned to me and said, "I love this about us. Most couples would be tearing each other's heads off right now, but we are just here, chillin', makin' the most of it. It is what it is."

(*It is what it is* is Garrett's favorite line which he quotes—and means—often.)

We settled for pizza at home that night with Henley, and it became a great first date story.

As Eddie Veddar sings in our song, *Future Days*, "When hurricanes and cyclones rage when wind turned dirt to dust, when floods they came or tides they raised ever closer became us. I believe, and I believe 'cause I can see our future days, days of you and me."

Doesn't Veddar's voice just spoon you? (Love me some Veddar!)

He is my garret, my live-in comedian, and the Ron Swanson to my Leslie Knope (if there were no Ben).

We are equal partners with complimentary personalities, collectively gathering our grit, and offering each other grace as we grow closer to the people whom God made us to be.

REAL WEDDING VOWS

A blog post from February 12, 2019

I'm sorry that I suck sometimes.

I'm sorry that I talk more than I listen,
And that I shrink all of your favorite shirts.

I'm sorry that I'm selfish and stubborn,
And miss out on opps to celebrate and learn from you.

I'm sorry that I make you my punching bag
when I feel beat up by the world.

I seek your forgiveness, will aim to move differently
and from death to us part,
I will live from a place of gratitude for you.

Thank you for forgiving me on days that I suck.

Thank you for encouraging me to be a better listener.

Thank you for wearing the now-tiny shirt to make me laugh.

Thank you for seeing my selfishness for what it truly is,
and reminding me that I'm not the only one
who is taking care of me now.

Thank you for celebrating my stubborn nature
when it is healthy and looks more like "determination."

Thank you for a wisdom that is so complimentary to mine.

I adore learning from and with you.

Thank you for rubbing my shoulders in the corner
of the boxing ring when the world beats me
up and telling me to get back out there.

Sometimes I see my daughter as our love incarnate. I look at her and think, "Look at our love. Just bouncing around in such loud beauty and wonder. Look at our love taking every opportunity to learn and to grow. Could there be a greater symbol of our love than she?"

Parenthood will be our final human relationship to explore in this longer-than-necessary-chapter on being known by God and others.

DESPITE THIS, THANK YOU.

A blog post from May 1, 2014

"It takes a village to raise a child—and always has. Though every child needs a mother, it is mothering we really need, since so many people must automatically be part of it. Every step along the way a child needs a responsible adult looking out for them, paving the way, being there when the crying begins and the bus number has been forgotten and the fear sets in. Mother's day is for all—we are all meant to mother the next generation." (Joan Chittister)

I have never valued my village more.

Their presence is truly life-giving. In my community, I find who God made me to be. I am 7 weeks and 5 days pregnant, and as a carrier of trisomy-13, I am *desperately* relying on the peace of the Holy Spirit that they bring.

The genetic counselor and doctors inform us that it's a good sign that the baby has made it this far, but I'm still nervous. If the results come back as positive, they have suggested a therapeutic termination to protect us both.

Lord, if I may be so selfish, if I may be so bold, save the baby that is growing inside of me.

It feels *so* egotistical to type this prayer. It feels so self-serving to lament this way. My good friend has given me a pep-talk to which I will now adhere. She has instructed me to celebrate—to celebrate the life that exists *now.* This is a difficult task for me. It is uncomfortable to write and speak of such things. To speak of them gives them life. To speak of them makes them a reality that I must face. To speak of them makes them a reality for which I might one day grieve.

Writing plainly, celebrating the life within me is *really* hard.

But alas, it should be celebrated.

Bring out the balloons! Bring out the streamers!

It is life that will live on regardless to how the CVS test goes on May 27th. I believe in life after death, I believe in everlasting life found in Christ.

There is peace in this realization—magnificent peace.

I believe that God loves this little blueberry-shaped creature more than Garrett and I combined. And while all I want is to sing and rock a little baby on 12/13/14, there currently is a 15% chance that this might not be the case, on earth, that is.

My views of God's providential care are being rocked by this notion. However, one thing is for certain. In the midst of life's uncomfortable mysteries, GOD IS WORKING FOR THE GOOD. This carries me and helps me maintain my sanity.

Along with this mantra, my heart proclaims an earth-shattering "thank you!"

Within my womb is a piece of Garrett and piece of me. Within my womb is a miracle. God is wonderfully knitting together a heart, a brain, limbs, and even a soul. What more is there to say but "_____." I stand speechless. I stand in awe of this miracle. Eyes and heart widened at my humanly attempt to comprehend this divine phenomenon.

Thank you. Thank you. Thank you. Despite the test results, thank you, God. For every grace-filled day, for every person that has ever loved me. For every beautiful sight and life-giving memory, and for the *miracle* that I am honored to carry—thank you.

A TOAST TO MOTHERHOOD

A toast I gave at my awesome Saturday Night Live-Themed Baby Shower by my friends in November of 2014.

Here Ye, Here Ye—I would like to make a toast.

Utter honor and excitement has filled my being since hearing word of this shower. I have felt a bit unworthy for such an unconventionally AMAZING shower. As I began to ponder ways to express my appreciation, hostess thank you gifts would just not do, so I thought, "Hmm, I shall write a speech; for nothing keeps a late-night party going like a powerful moment of prose!" As all of you know, I am a talker. I feel and share love the most through words, so in advance—you are welcome.

My heart overflows with gratitude towards the hostesses, to all of you, and the resiliently dynamic woman whom I call, "mom."

To our fantastic hostesses, I proclaim, "THANK YOU!" These decorations, grub, games, invites and the numerous mind-blowingly creative brainstorming sessions led to a top-notch night with friends that will be forever treasured.

Abbie: To the band-nerd, Jesus-freak that lived across my hall freshman year, I say thank you. Your level of humility is a mismatch for the high level of wit and intellect that you possess.

Your level of selfless compassion is second to none. I respect how emotionally invested you are in every conversation. Many times, I am not aware of my own feelings towards matters, until I notice you tearing up about them as I share. I pray to be half the helpful giver that you are.

Lindsay: My first real friend, my college roommate, and the one that truly deserves a party tonight for putting up with me for four years. You have always had the uncanny ability to beautifully balance rest, work, and play while encouraging others to make a positive difference in their community. I have been learning from you for years. You create an adventure wherever you go. Thank you for always allowing me to tag along for the ride.

Lauren: The professional hard-ass with a heart-of-gold. Lauren. Gets. Stuff. Done. I admire the heck out of someone who can be such an intimidating, efficient presence in a business meeting one minute then giggling on the back of a crashing tube the next. I am so thankful for the similarities in our stories. To share the same "3/achiever" lens with you benefits me in my attempt to process my world. Thank you. Your skills in business/marketing are like magic tricks that will forever leave me stumped and in awe from the audience below.

Leah: Who knew two gals who labeled each other as "fake" nine years ago would grow such a life-giving professional and personal relationship. I am daily blessed by your boldness and lovingly prophetic voice. We are wired very differently. This makes for some complimentary dynamics at meetings. Thank you for reading my facial expressions so well, even when I think I am hiding my true opinion—you get me. You keep me humble while also empowering me to be me.

Now onto the rest of the guests—JUST KIDDING! I know we want to get back to the fun, so in closing, allow me to make seven more points.

I am so grateful that this is the time that God is blessing me with Henley June. I honestly feel all of our paths were meant to cross BEFORE I became a mother. In so many unique ways, you all have showered my life with wisdom, joy, and peace. It is this mighty community of women that I discovered my identity. You have each taught me to feel, to forgive, and to love. I hold a much more celebratory view of life because of the kindred spirits in this space. Thank you.

Your friendship has been one of God's greatest gifts to me, and I should have been paying you because it healed me more than therapy and self-help books. That's right, I said it. This attempt at a whole person (plus 1) that stands before you tonight is mostly due to your healing friendship. Henley will have a much healthier and happier mother because of *you*. Thank you for allowing Christ to work through you in such a transformative way.

As the wise nun, who never had children, Joan Chitistter wrote, "Mothering has many aspects but two are central: birthing the child physically and caring for their needs once they're born. But only one of these can be done by one woman. The rest can be shared by many and <u>must</u> be if we are all to be fully developed human beings. So, within this village, child-raising is a creative endeavor; it is an art of many, it is an art rather than a science."

Thus, let us raise our glasses to the babies of our wombs and the babies of our world. We toast tonight to all of those who mothered us and the many ways we are privileged to mother others.

CHEERS!

BLISTERS

I don't drink too much.

I wouldn't go as far as to say that I drink like a Baptist in hiding, and I most *certainly* don't drink like a Catholic. I would say that I drink like an upper-class Lutheran. So, when it comes to a wedding, there is nothing I love more than a dainty vodka cranberry or three and then *tearing up* the dance floor. (Vodka speeds up your metabolism, so it's basically a superfood.)

Many a DJ have been annoyed by me obnoxiously shouting out such classics as "Wobble, Wobble," "Boot Scootin' Boogie," or "Dougie" *until* said songs are played. I will out dance any-one—*anyone*, and usually around the third hour, my heels are getting the best of me, and I finally acknowledge my well-earned "Single Lady" blisters.

But how can I stop dancing?!

While I'm uncomfortably in pain, I'm having *way* too much fun to stop and "Cotton Eye Joe" just started playing. I push through and dance another thirty minutes or so. I gleefully jig through my hurt, and have *no* regrets for the Band-Aids and soreness that await me in the morning. It was *all* worth it.

This scenario perfectly describes what it's like in the first few months of being a parent (minus the vodka).

While I felt completely uncomfortable at times (due to a lack of sleep, and increased anxiety), any displeasure was overshadowed by pure and utter love, and awe. All of the feelings coexisted of course, but just like my glee for "Cupid Shuffle" keeps me and my blisters on the dance floor, the sheer honor of being a parent carried me through my discomfort.

As numerous emotions coincided within me, I was reminded of how the words "sacred" and "scared" hold the same letters.

Isn't this fascinating?

With my funky chromosomes, those nine-months were full of moments in which I was both *fully* scared, while also *fully* aware of the sacred that was at work within me. I fully submitted to playing a role in this divine act and committed as charged by the poet, Ruth Thompson,

"I give my body over
To nurturing this life,
I give my warmth, my blood, my bones,
I give my peace, my patience,
My rest, my energy.
I ask God for thoughts of joy
To soothe and comfort me."[15]

Every day during my pregnancy, I would sing (something I do often) a song of praise in Crowder's, "How He Loves Us," as my mantra. This idea of sinking in an ocean of healing grace was just what I and my delicate zygote needed. These lyrics carried me, although for some reason during the pains of childbirth, my personal playlist changed to off-key belting of "She'll be Coming Around the Mountain" and "Holy Night." (Ridiculously annoying to the nurses, of that I am sure.)

It was a glorious Thanksgiving, when Henley June made her debut. Seeing as how I knew I would only get to do this unbelievably-sacred-awesome thing once, I felt *beyond* privileged that not only did my water break, but also that the hospital was a ghost town. Garrett and I were pleasantly surprised to see so few people. While we had loads of family in town, they were all thankfully asleep at 4 a.m. Everything outside of me was calm and quiet, but inside, my apprehension was speaking up.

---

15   Norton, Joan; *14 Steps to Awaken the Sacred Feminine,* 118-19.

My blood pressure was through the roof. Add to this, four nurses who, "Can always get it in," failed to get my IV in. Finally, an angel from on high in a paramedic costume named Neil appeared and without me even feeling a thing, got my IV in. This was a small omen to me, since my dad is a firefighter/paramedic, and he and my Mom had yet to arrive from their home seven hours away. Garrett and I would tell tales of the mighty Neil for years to come.

Between the time that my water broke at 3:30 a.m. and 8:37 p.m. when she introduced herself, there were many laughable moments. My midwife, who I adored, was only going to be out of town one day that month, and it was Thanksgiving. With this said, another OB, who also happened to be a member of the church I served would be doing the delivery. Thankfully, he was a Swede who couldn't care less about missing the turkey.

Now while this might have bothered some moms, it made my heart smile. When he came in at around 10:30 a.m. to highly suggest Pitocin, he brought his 4-year-old daughter with him. His kids were highly involved in our ministerial programs, so seeing her was a pleasant distraction. He placed her on a stool up by my face, and she and I shared grins. (My bottom half was covered the entire time she was in there.)

He must have known that she was just what I needed, and that intuition was one reason that he was the perfect doctor for us.

Seeing as how it was Thanksgiving, we were able to watch the *Macy's Day* parade and the *Pedigree Dog Show* as the Pitocin kicked in. I also got to watch Garrett enjoy stuffing from the hospital cafeteria. I don't know how I missed it, but I never recall being told that I couldn't eat while in labor and this was by far the most painful part of my day. If I would've known that, gorging the day before would've been a must.

The Pitocin finally did kick in with fury and it was at this time that I became very appreciative of Garrett's ingenuity. He had brought a hand-held robotic massager, and after an hour of massaging my lower back, he removed his belt and strapped the massager onto my back. It. Was. Hilarious.

And, most importantly, it worked.

I desperately needed a robotic massager attached to me, because the epidural dude was on vacation (like the rest of the world, or so it felt like in that vacant hospital).

After a long, painful wait, another epidural dude was found and I was proud of myself for making it to a seven before he had arrived. Getting an epidural is quite the bonding experience for you and your spouse. For that reason alone, I would highly recommend it. Garrett lovingly hoisted my achy body into a seated position on the side of the bed and then I leaned *all* of my body weight onto him as the epidural dude inserted a thick-ole needle into my lower back. I cried and snorted as he patted my upper back and reminded me of my strength.

I then requested enchiladas and fell asleep while my body continued to do its thing. Isn't that fascinating that the body will continue contracting while sleeping?

Nice work, God.

When the time had finally arrived for me to push, Garrett was an excellent coach. So much so, that the nurse on my left-leg realized it and said early-on, "You know what? I'm going to stop counting, and let your husband count and guide your breaths and pushes."

And he did. It's funny, when he and I were in parenting classes, the idea of a mirror over the delivery bed was the furthest thing from desirable. But, when the time came, we both wanted to see as much of the miracle as possible. (Yes, Dear

Reader Friend, if you have yet to procreate, you might find that gross. I know I did before I got knocked-up.)

Sadly, I was asked to remove my glasses, so I could barely see the mirror, but it was still an OK visual guide for my pushing. With Garrett on my right-leg guiding my breaths and pushes, we soon brought forth our little life-force. I can still feel the pushes, but my favorite memory to replay is the one of the Doctor putting her on my chest.

Her eyes were ginormous. She was perfect. Like a little Martian absorbing earth for the first time, those eyes were filled with wonder and gunk. (So. Much. Gunk.) She fit so perfectly in my neck-nook as Garrett and I both kissed her wittle head.

"It's so nice to meet you, Henley June," I said to her, but this really wasn't our first encounter. I figured there was no more appropriate reaction than to sing her the song that she had heard on repeat since she had been conceived, so I sang her Crowder's "How He Loves Us" over and over and over again during that first hour of cuddles. "He is jealous for me. Loves like a hurricane and we are the trees bending beneath the weight of his grace and mercy…Then heaven meets earth, with an unforeseen kiss… If grace is an ocean, we're all sinking."

We three were truly sinking in an ocean of grace, and couldn't be more thankful.

As we got home, as it usually does, the euphoric love faded, and fear became loud again.

Could Garrett and I handle this?

A STONED JAMES FRANCO

My mom joined us on my maternity leave to hourly douse the house with bleach and passively bring me fruit per my request for ice cream. Thankfully I was not deprived for long, for as soon as Garrett's Mom arrived, she baked up a storm. Homemade cinnamon rolls, cakes, and twice-baked potatoes adorn my memories because of her. Both types of help, the cleaning and the cooking, were truly appreciated.

We had Henley in a cradle next to our bed for a spell, when I was waking up often to nurse. Thanks to Garrett, my nightstand was full of snacks, drinks, Lanolin. He also hotwired switches on the wall so that the lamp across the room could be turned on with ease. This was around the time that the anti-climactic Franco and Rogan film, *The Interview* was coming out, so *Pineapple Express* was on repeat on *Comedy Central*. I'd never seen that academy award-worthy film before, and now I have watched it too many times to count.

So, there we were; me, a stoned James Franco and a Martian on a mission—feed said Martian and return her to sleep. Garrett would awake with us sometimes, but sadly his paternity leave was much shorter than my maternity leave. If only we could be more like Canada.

At the cue of her cry, I would get her out of the crib and lay her on the bed in front of me while I adjusted my *very* attractive nursing bra. I would look at her small, feeble body, and think, *Wow, this is truly amazing that I get to help grow you. Can I do this? Can we do this? What if you get hurt? What if someone hurts you? What if I'm a bad example for you? What if I push you too hard? Or not enough? (Hah! That's not possible!) What if you choose bad friends? What if you wear clothes that don't match? What if I feed you Red Dye #40?*

And then I would pick her up to nurse, and God's gift of oxytocin would calm my inner storm. I would look at those awe-filled eyes and the fear would have nothing left to say. In those 3 a.m. nursing sessions, I felt similarly to what Trent Wagler of the band the Steel Wheels does as he sings to his daughter,

> "One night you were a princess in a town that knows its age
> We sat and watched the music and the colors on the stage
> We leaned and swayed together humming one another's tune
> You fell asleep upon me like you could cure all my wounds,
> Like you cure all my wounds."

There is truly something healing about becoming a parent, and I feel I'm just on the brink of its main lessons. There are wounds to heal, values to be realigned, and lots of take-home points in this uncertain, yet comforting; scared, but sacred time.

9 LESSONS FROM MY 90-DAY-OLD

A blog post from February 28, 2015

1. **Parenting is not a competitive sport, it's a relationship.** Our high amounts of parenting books and blogs ranging from all sorts of philosophies, have occasionally left me out-of-breath in my attempts to raise the smartest, best-fed, well-rested child. This is not healthy for my personality type. The pre-existing pressure I put on myself far surpasses that of the world's. A healthier route I have found is to view this life-changing endeavor as a beautiful relationship. From this angle, there are: preferences, personalities, and inside jokes. There are compromises, boundaries, and mistakes. Here, there is a fluid flow to each day and a forever amount of grace. From this perspective of parenting, the mutual love of all parties involved quiets down the annoying voice within that whispers, "You are not doing it *right*."

2. **Be aware of the "black & white" rules, but trust your intuition in the "gray" areas.** My husband and I nervously *Googled* all of the black & white rules of having a newborn. How many ounces she should drink in a 24-hour period? 24. Prescribed room temperature to decrease the chance of SIDS? 68-72. Are two examples enough? Yes. Subjective rules such as these are best when whole-heartedly followed. However, some grey areas have arisen. Here, my personal readings of Henley have led to a different/better solution than that of my parenting books. I am learning to trust myself in my love-filled knowledge of my daughter.

3. **Domestic tasks can become sacred.** This lesson I am borrowing from the wise ole' French monk, Brother Lawrence. In the book, *Practicing the Presence of God*, he writes of disciplining himself to experience simple chores around the monastery as worship. I was surprised at how quickly my sometimes emotionally unavailable, task-oriented self-found nursing as a form of worship. I would play my favorite Bebo Norman tracks and rock away to the highest heavens. Not only nursing, but also hand-washing onesies and lugging around the heaviest of carriers—all have become very holy to me. I realize this euphoric state is possibly fleeting; now I relish in the joy of the mundane.

4. **Celebrate the different seasons of Life.** As a mother who works outside of the home, I quickly noticed that I have yet to feel completely back at work. I am there physically, but the innovative mindset I usually work out of has yet to return. I am rolling by in maintenance mode. My wonderful supervisor informed me that the majority of the ecclesial year is set in what is known as "ordinary time." High and

holy days (holidays) exist but not always. My creative passion will return to work at some point, but in this season of life, it is totally permissible to be utterly obsessed with my newborn daughter-as long as I don't drop the ball too much at work.

5. **Life Callings *can* coexist.** I have been so very blessed. I have flexible work hours and my new office-mate is my three-month-old. Thanks to a magnificent team, my husband's work schedule, and an experimental mindset this set up has far surpassed my expectations. During the first portion of my maternity leave, I was over-dramatically hesitant to return to work. I was then saved by the modest revelation (once I was back for three weeks) that every child in our programs was either A) someone else's Henley or B) needed someone to love him/her the way I love Henley. In the United Methodist Church, we talk about "callings." One can be called by the Holy Spirit into a relationship or into a certain vocation. I feel God has called me into the ministries of marriage, motherhood, and serving the children of our community through the local church.

6. **Happiness is not always the aim.** We Christians, especially those of us who serve in the local church, are often guilty of what I call 'Ned-Flanders-Syndrome'. As you may know, he is an overly positive, Holy Roller on *The Simpsons*. He would aim to deny all feelings that were opposite of happiness. He acted in a way that anger and sadness would make him less faithful. This is clearly not true or healthy. My three month old has confirmed an alternative option. Our *Parents as First Teachers* coach informed us that an infant's only way to release emotionally after a long day of mental stimulation

is to cry. She advised that we allow this to occur. (In fact, she encouraged it!) She guided us to swaddle tightly and invite her to "let-it-go" within the tension of the *Halo*. This would be very cathartic for her. Angrily grunting, sadly crying, and joyfully laughing are <u>all</u> recommended for one's development.

7. **Trust your spouse's gifts and honor his/her limits.** While our parenting philosophies are 99% the same, we are good at different parts of parenting. I'd say we are both equally skilled at reading her, consoling her, and purely enjoying the heck out of being with her. My husband takes home the gold in any and all of the logistical details of parenting. Being able to jump into action at the drop of a hat and manage many parental tasks at once—now that's my forte. It would not benefit our family in any way if I were to alter my wiring and live out of his areas of giftedness and vice versa. Furthermore, it is helpful to no one for me to hover while Garrett is with her and passively correct him.

8. **There is a difference between "being responsible for" and "being in control of."** Due to our broken world and free-will, I cannot control all that Henley's life will entail. (#heartache) I cannot control how others will treat her or her choices. This worries me, because like all parents I want her to be as happy and as safe as possible. I have no real control over her, yet her father and I are 100% responsible for her (at this phase any way). All that I can control are my reactions to what life throws at me and I pray I can pass this realization on to Henley. I find comfort in this lack of control through faith. I know before Henley June was mine, she was God's. I know that although her father and I love

her with an unsurpassable love, God's love surpasses ours. I know that God is at work for the good in her life regardless of her future choices, regardless of the broken world in which she lives. As one with "helicopter mom" tendencies, I am still grappling with this lesson. The good news is that since I have no real control over her choices, I can't be blamed when she TPs her principal's house in high school, right?!

9. **Remain in the miracle mentality.** As mentioned before, my chromosomes are connected in a funky way. To speak in medical terms, I have a Robertsonian translocation between my 13th and 22nd chromosome. With this said, Henley June is a reality that I was uncertain would ever exist. My situation is not unique really; for all babies are miracles. During my pregnancy, it was so easy for me to daily be in awe of the miracle that my husband and I were co-creating with God. This was probably the rush of hormones, but none-the-less, each day I lived out of a miracle mentality. As the years pass, I momentarily take one step further down the mountain, and I become a little less in awe of the entire experience of birthing and raising a miracle. My goal is to look at Henley the same when she is eighteen as I did when I first saw her waving to me on that ultra-sound monitor. I want to eternally see her as a miracle—a miracle that I am so honored to raise.

OF THE PUBLIC

While there is much to learn as a parent, there, as usual, is just as much at which to laugh. For instance, as my pregnancy became more apparent among our parishioners, some took it upon themselves to visit me in my office with bits of prenatal advice.

One of my most beloved Methodist matriarchs in our church family would poke her head in and say, "How are you feeling today?"

I would look up from my computer and say, "Pretty well. She's moving a lot, and I have some acid reflux, but overall, I am well."

With a look of epiphany on her face, she would proclaim, "Acid reflux huh? Well, you know what cures that, don't you? Losing five pounds!" and then she would politely walk away.

Losing five pounds seemed to be her suggestion for every ailment in life, pregnant or not, she would kindly suggest this to everyone. It was like Windex in the comedy, "My Big Fat Greek Wedding," just much more offensive.

Another beloved matriarch in our tribe waited for me in the foyer following my sermon, (Side Sermon: Preaching while pregnant is the *most sublime* thing ever. It's as if your arsenal of Holy has been temporarily doubled. It's as if your child is chaperoning *you* on the field trip of the sermon.)

"I want to commend you for buying prenatal clothes during this season, Meg," she said in an unintentionally pretentious tone. "You are a woman about town, or should I say, a woman of the public, and your appearance most certainly matters at times like these."

I diplomatically smiled and thanked her for her compliment although I felt like I had fallen into a time portal when I heard it. *Woman of the public?!*

Being in her eighties, she seemed to be extremely curious about our career plans after Henley arrived. When I shared with her that Garrett and I would arrange our hours at work to where she would be with one of us while the other was at work, she said excitingly, "Oh, my, Meg, this truly is a post-modern world, isn't it? Your husband is so progressive taking a different shift for your child *and* doing diapers and feedings. Henri and I were not that way at all, but I am so glad things are changing for parents these days. The roles really are changing for the better."

While the institution of the church might have *many* areas of growth, the most beautiful human need that it meets better than other organizations is that of intergenerational connections, and these two women are prime examples of that. Meeting this need will also be vital for our Gen Z kids as we assist them in navigating technology and relearning conversational tactics. I am excited to see how the church evolves to better meet this need.

For this new working mom, our church staff worked diligently to meet my needs. I was able to bring Henley to work with me for a bit, and they would put signs on my office door when she was napping. My co-worker applied for a grant in which we received a mini-fridge in my office for breast-milk. They also put signs up on my door to avoid awkward interruptions while pumping. I will be *forever* grateful for this.

Whilst Garrett and the church helped ease my anxiety of childcare, and I was privileged that nursing worked out well for us three, the biggest lesson I had to learn (and am still learning) was around boundaries between my work and home life. And since this called for a mentality shift, no one could figure this out but me.

Boards and committees that used to be of high importance to me, no longer mattered after Henley was born. So I got off of *all* of them. I figured if something was going to keep me away from her, it better be aligned with my vocational calling, or be a crap-ton of fun.

Like most new parents, our lives got super simplified post-birth. Garrett worked nights for her first three years, and she and I were rarely out past 6 p.m. I most likely annoyed many because I was *so* strict on my rule of "no meetings after 5 p.m." I know it sounds ludicrous, but it was doable. Whenever I was being "a woman about town" with her, I made a point to never talk about work—with anyone. Taking these steps was uber helpful to me in being a present parent, but like with most rules, an exception soon emerges.

During the heat of the summer, Henley and I packed up our swim bag and headed to the city pool. The VFW was doing a free swim day and cook out, so the place was packed. Due to the free meal, the majority were people that I knew from our community meal and utility assistance program. I was tempted to turn back and persuade her to settle for sprinklers in the yard, but I stayed the course. I could stay present with her while being surrounded by people I serve at work, right?

Wrong.

Not a moment after we plopped down on the side of the toddler pool, a young mom holding a pre-mature infant came and sat by us. Being a member of a low-income family that we had helped often in our church office, I had known this particular mom since she was in middle school and did not mind her joining us. But I wanted to try my best to not put back on my work hat because rules are meant to be followed (at all cost). I would *not* talk about work while playing with Henley.

The mom chatted about her new job, and her sister's dating drama while I held her adorable baby. She, like all of us, was sweating, so Henley and I gently patted water on her tiny legs and noggin. Henley was enamored with the miniscule creature in my arms. It was so inspiring to watch. Halfway through the conversation, the mom asked me if I could help her find quality childcare for her kids. Her boyfriend was in prison for a bit, and the Department of Children and Families was apparently on her case to get a plan in place while she was at work.

My heart broke for the little love in my arms. I did not know that the DCF was involved in her family's life, but I guess it made sense. I looked at Henley who was still dripping water on the infant's legs, and I knew it was time for me to break my own rule. It was time for me to put my work hat back on and help this little gal, by helping her momma.

I reached behind me and pulled out my wallet with business cards and a pen and paper. I got intentional in my conversation with the mom and gave her contact info for all of the resources in our area. At one point while I was writing, Henley wanted me to go and slide with her, and I had to say the words that my mouth detests, "I'm sorry, baby, I can't play right now." But this time these soured words were followed with, "This little baby needs help finding someone to care for her while her mommy works. And I promise I will move fast and then come slide with you." She seemed to understand, and then jostled over to some other tots on the slide.

As soon as I had wrapped up the conversation with the mom, I ran (as fast as one could in one-foot of water) over to Henley and played with her for the next two hours.

A small amount of guilt came over me as we drove home, I was so mad that I had not honored my work/home boundary. I kept peering back at her through the rearview mirror to see if the scars I had given her were noticeable yet. She just grinned back and belted the lyrics of *Let It Go*. I made a vow then to do better at following my own rules.

After dinner, baths, and stories we sat in her blue rocking chair, and began to pray. Per our usual routine, I asked her what she wanted to thank God for that day. Without missing a beat, she said, "Mom, we need to be sure and pray for that little baby—that she finds a nice babysitter to take care of her."

I was shocked. How could this little three-year-old who was obsessed with the slide even remember that? What an unexpected level of empathy! I felt a lump in my throat and I said, "You're exactly, right, Henley, we do need to pray for that little baby." And we did, while I ugly-cried.

Sometimes our rules are selfish.

Even if they're not selfish, the motives of our rules need to occasionally be revaluated.

Here I was trying to protect my own relationship with my daughter (which is all well and good) while there was another child who desperately needed to be included in our relationship. If I had honored my rule, not only would I have not been helpful to that family, but Henley would have also been denied the joy of caring and praying for another. I was so fearful of my daughter seeing me with my work-hat on, that I almost robbed her of the opportunity to see me using my talents (I'm known as the "I know a guy" gal.) to serve others, i.e., the greatest lesson I want to pass down to her. Henley recalls that day at the pool with glee, and that inspires me toward a greater flexibility in my own rules, especially when relationships are at stake.

THE WELL

Regardless of the tier of relationship, our connection with others is what carries us closer to the healing love of our Creator.

As taught in 1 John 4:12, our relationships with God and others are interconnected. While certain friendships seem to be more infused with holy love than others, *all* interactions have the potential to point toward God. In some way or another, they can carry us toward the greatest love of all; the love of a God who made us, knows us and loves us. And it would be remissive of me to wrap up this section on relationships without addressing our relationship with God.

This key connection is very evident in the encounter of Jesus and the woman at the well in John 4:1-30.

"Now when Jesus learned that the Pharisees had heard, "Jesus is making and baptizing more disciples than John" —although it was not Jesus himself but his disciples who baptized— he left Judea and started back to Galilee. But he had to go through Samaria. So he came to a Samaritan city called Sychar, near the plot of ground that Jacob had given to his son Joseph. Jacob's well was there, and Jesus, tired out by his journey, was sitting by the well.

It was about noon.

A Samaritan woman came to draw water, and Jesus said to her, "Give me a drink." (His disciples had gone to the city to buy food.) The Samaritan woman said to him, "How is it that you, a Jew, ask a drink of me, a woman of Samaria?" (Jews do not share things in common with Samaritans.) Jesus answered her, "If you knew the gift of God, and who it is that is saying to you, 'Give me a drink,' you would have asked him, and he would have given you living water."

The woman said to him, "Sir, you have no bucket, and the well is deep. Where do you get that living water? Are you greater than our ancestor Jacob, who gave us the well, and with his sons and his flocks drank from it?" Jesus said to her, "Everyone who drinks of this water will be thirsty again, but those who drink of the water that I will give them will never be thirsty. The water that I will give will become in them a spring of water gushing up to eternal life." The woman said to him, "Sir, give me this water, so that I may never be thirsty or have to keep coming here to draw water."

Jesus said to her, "Go, call your husband, and come back." The woman answered him, "I have no husband." Jesus said to her, "You are right in saying, 'I have no husband'; for you have had five husbands, and the one you have now is not your husband. What you have said is true!" The woman said to him, "Sir, I see that you are a prophet. Our ancestors worshiped on this mountain, but you say that the place where people must worship is in Jerusalem."

Jesus said to her, "Woman, believe me, the hour is coming when you will worship the Father neither on this mountain nor in Jerusalem. You worship what you do not know; we worship what we know, for salvation is from the Jews. But the hour is coming, and is now here, when the true worshipers will worship the Father in spirit and truth, for the Father seeks such as these to worship him. God is spirit, and those who worship him must worship in spirit and truth." The woman said to him, "I know that Messiah is coming" (who is called Christ). "When he comes, he will proclaim all things to us." Jesus said to her, "I am he, the one who is speaking to you."

Just then his disciples came. They were astonished that he was speaking with a woman, but no one said, "What do you want?" or, "Why are you speaking with her?" Then the woman left her water jar and went back to the city. She said to the people, "Come and see a man who told me everything I have ever done! He cannot be the Messiah, can he?" They left the city and were on their way to him.

Do you think she had any idea what the day would hold when she awoke that morning?

What are the odds that the same time she was retrieving water, would be the same exact time that Jesus decided to take a breather on his trip to Galilee? This scene is painted beautifully in the testimony of John. Jesus was alone. His disciples had ventured to find lunch, so there he sat by the well.

He asked for water. This left her shocked, not because she was a woman, but more importantly, because of their religious differences. Due to noon not being the most popular time to retrieve water from the well, chances are there were not many others around. With this, she called him on it, "How come You, a Jew, are asking me, a Samaritan, for a drink?"

He answered her, "If you knew the generosity of God and who I am, you would be asking Me for a drink, and I would give you fresh, *living* water." As one would guess, this response of Jesus led the woman to doubt and refute him with sound arguments. This should not surprise us that she was capable to discuss the origin of the well so comfortably with a Jewish man, for in contrast to the Rabbinic law exempting women from certain observances—Samaritans did not make any distinctions between [genders] in reference to their common obligation to carry out the Law. Due to the Samaritans interpreting the Pentateuch strictly, the injunction of Deuteronomy 31:12 indicates that the Samaritan practice of educating children of both sexes in the law and Samaritan traditions probably dates back to their origins.

She knew her faith's foundation, and probably fed up with the pharisaic traditions, she was more than ready to reject the words of "this Jew." In hopes of never having to come back to this well again, she simply gave in and requested this "living water" He spoke of. He then said something unexpected. He revealed to her that He knew of her five husbands and that the man she was living with now was not her husband.

He knew her.

How could he have known that? She thought. *A prophet?!* She then continued on with her questioning and inspecting His thoughts on the differences in worship between the Jews and the Samaritans. In the bustle of her own words, she almost allowed the words of Jesus to float right over her head. Perhaps Jesus slightly interrupted her a bit and said, "The time is coming-in fact it has come-when where you worship will not matter. It's who you are and the way that you live that count before God... That's the kind of people the Father is looking for: those who are simply and honestly themselves before Him." (Message, John 4:22-24)

The woman replied, "Well I don't know about that. I do *know* though that the Messiah is coming." She took another drink of water. "I am He," Jesus responded. "You don't have to wait any longer or look any further."

As the disciples returned, shocked to see Him speaking with a woman, something He hadn't done since the wedding at Cana in John 2, the Samaritan woman became uncomfortable and ran back to the village. She proclaimed to everyone, "Come see the Man who KNEW all about the things I did. He knows me inside and out!"

One of the finest spiritual writers of our time, Henri Nouwen once wrote,

> "For most of my life, I had struggled to...*know God*...I have tried hard to follow the guidelines of the spiritual life, pray always, work for others, read the scriptures—to avoid the many temptations to dissipate myself. I have failed many times but always tried again, even when I was close to despair. Now I wonder whether I have sufficiently realized that during all this time God has been *trying to know me*.

The question is not, "How am I to know God?" but "How am I to let myself be known by God?"[16]

The God who made us, loves us, *and continues to make us daily takes great initiative to know us deeper.* Though sometimes we hide from God, or we are very selective as to what we choose to reveal. In our brokenness, we retreat in isolation from a loving community. Or in the competitive world we live in, we hide behind our talents or accomplishments, praying and hoping that no one will ever discover who we *truly* are, what we *truly* think, how weak we can sometimes be.

With a smile on our face, we secretly doubt our own inner goodness. "Instead of experiencing their outward success as a sign of their inner Beauty," Nouwen teaches, "they live them as a cover-up for their sense of personal worthlessness." [17] But oh, if we only could wrap our hearts around how *very* much God not only loves us but achingly yearns to know us deeper. If it weren't for the unconditional love of my top-tier folks, I would still be hiding behind my talents, where I was forbidden from fully knowing myself, others, and God.

But, it's not just the top-tier folks who get the credit.

It's taken the life-giving *and* life-sucking interactions of *all* my different relational tiers, to teach me that life has little to do with how much I know *about* God, and more to do with my efforts to know others as God knows them (even if this only leads to a Christ-like tolerance). Instead of impressing others with my knowledge of God, maybe I should be concerned about how well I'm allowing God to know me.

---

16   Nouwen; *The Return of the Prodigal Son: A Story of Homecoming*, 106.

17   Ibid., 108.

And in tapping into this knowledge, I find the life I was meant to live.

I am my own sanctuary.

*My being houses the Holy. Grit
and grace come from within,
regardless of the choices of others.*

*My body is beautiful;
a gift that should be cared for,
trusted, and never feared.*

*My mind is uniquely mine.
While it is ever-expanding,
I call the shots on its focus,
stillness, and creativity.*

*My emotions are all necessary
and should be embraced.*

*My spirit was made for
a relationship with God and others.*

AS YOU FORGE ONWARD AS YOUR OWN SANCTUARY, ASK YOURSELF:

1. How would you compare knowing *about* God, knowing God, and *being known* by God?

2. Is there a Tier 3 relationship into which you are mistakenly pouring a Tier 1 amount of work (and it's leaving you miserable)? What is a boundary that you are comfortable creating with this person? Could that happen this week? Will that happen this week?

3. Although Tier 1 relationships bring you much life with very little effort, you and that person are both better off by investing in one another. What percent of your week is spent with/on your Tier 1 relationships? Is this enough to help you sustain the life-sucking sorcery of those Tier 3 relationships? What routine could you establish that will keep you more connected to a certain Tier 1 relationship?

CHAPTER SIX

Serving From My Soul: The First Disciple's Courage

MY TOP 10 LIST OF
WHY BEING A MINISTER IS WEIRD

Blog post from April 30, 2018

1. People think that all ministers are like Ned Flanders from the *Simpsons* and are capable of only one emotion—oblivious glee.

2. It is assumed that you live like an Amish-nun (not a thing, but a funny image!) and are not up-to-date on the current trends of fashion, entertainment, or technology.

3. Folks confuse necessary relational methods from a minister with a desire to be their new best friend. (I'm not your best friend, Carol!)

4. In honor of being nice and in the name of (how they are defining) "grace," churches sometimes discount (actual)

talent and emotional maturity when selecting volunteer leaders. This lack of standards can be a huge liability and end up hurting the entire team/tribe.

5. Never will there be a place where volunteers have *so* much power. This can be a good thing (priesthood of all believers and such) if the above point does not happen, but if it does, it will take a strong staff to do some major damage control.

6. Because all of our staff's job descriptions get blurred by our church members, sometimes blame is misplaced.

7. When you serve in a small town, some always think you are "on the clock." It takes years to teach folks how to treat you when you are at *Jose Peppers* with your family. (What?! Ministers eat chips and queso?! What?! Ministers leave the church?!)

8. It's so odd that some want their church to grow and be sustainable but are *highly* intolerant of the noise of kids and youth in the church. It's as if they don't see the connection between the two.

9. This won't apply to my Dear Reader Friends on the Coasts, but in the South and Midwest, there is still an odd stigma around alcohol, cussing and tattoos for ministers. That's *so* 1961. (And I'm *so* over it.)

10. Some were raised on translations of the Bible that were somehow filled with typos. Their versions were sadly void of the stories of Esther, Mary, Salome, and Lydia. I'm so sad for them because they have been misinformed and believe that women can't lead in the name of the

Lord. Occasionally running into these folks is most likely the weirdest thing about the gig. (Let it be known though, I preached my first sermon in the Bible belt, was a chaplain on the east coast, and served in the Midwest, and I have *never* run into this with members of my own tribe.) These people are out there though, and we really need to get 'em better versions of the Bible.

MOUNT SINAI

Jerusalem, Mount Sinai, and Lourdes, France are some of the world's most popular sacred sites. One housed the first temple and the cross, the other hosted the Ten Commandments, and the other apparently contains a grotto with healing water after Mary of Nazareth repeatedly revealed herself in the late nineteenth century. Each year, thousands visit to see if any of the holy that occurred remain.

God spoke in these places. Revelations were shared at these places. Heaven and earth touched at these places, and life was *never* the same.

Similar to one taking a pilgrimage to a sacred site, I believe that when one serves through his vocational calling, he has entered an internal sacred site—a sacred site within the soul. A sacred site is no longer just a destination to visit, but a *space* from which to live.

When you first tread on the path of the sacred site of your calling, time freezes while simultaneously flying by. As you witness others living out of a similar calling, it is a mystical hug. Like a crystal ball, you see that the future of your dreams *does* actually exist, and it's more glorious than you ever thought.

While you carry out the tasks of your calling, there's no competitive feeling in your bones because you're disinterested in being the best. You just want to *do* it for the pure bliss of doing it. You don't have to moderate your ambition because pride is not what drives you. Joy drives you. There's no rush to "arrive," because that would imply an ending, and you *never* want to stop doing *this thing* that you were made to do.

If you had to clean porta-potties four days a week with a toothbrush, just to do this thing on Friday, you would gleefully scrub Monday through Thursday, because that's how much life this type of work brings you.

Although it does not take you much work to do it well, you adore the craft so much that you eagerly pour countless hours into honing it. Others may wonder how it is that you understand this type of work and seem to "effortlessly" excel at it, and that is because it's not their calling, but it is (without a shadow of a doubt) yours.

Now that you have discovered the sacred site within that is your vocational calling, you pilgrimage there daily, and no other land compares. No other site satisfies.

At least this is how it feels for me, and I believe I first traveled there when I was six.

GOSPEL HYMNS

It would be my first Sunday to sing with the church choir, and my mom braided with pride. She had gotten me this "gig" through a friend at work, and I had earnestly been practicing. While the congregation was made up of all races, the choir members were all African-American adults who sang gospel hymns like there was no tomorrow. They lovingly welcomed me into their group and set a standard of *true* worship for me.

The choir loft and pews were white, and I quickly learned that the *only* way to sing was with ones whole body. We clapped and swayed, and on this first Sunday, I felt something I had never before felt. While I was being cradled by their songs, as John Wesley said, "my heart was strangely warmed," and I felt as though I was surrounded by the security of light. I felt at peace and I felt loved. In retrospect, it's clear to me that this was me tuning into the power of the Holy Spirit for the first time in my life. While God had always been with me, my first memory of an undeniable awareness of this was in that choir loft, singing those gospel hymns.

Being in a choir was always comforting to me, because success came easily to me there. It brought me a sense of worth early on that my 'D' report cards failed to do for some reason. I actually detested school until I met Mr. Spriggs in 2nd grade, and he, as my mom says, "changed everything for me."

He looked like Santa with a clean shave and was super-jolly to boot. Upon noticing how much I loved to write, he encouraged me to write Gospel hymns or long-winded stories for show and tell. He even told my mom that my gifts for words and wit could really take me places and that he would not be surprised at all if I became a comedian. *All* of this, he saw and affirmed in six-year-old Meg. I felt so loved and understood in his class, and this type of care would sustain me through the years ahead.

The years that followed brought more heartache to my family and to support us doing this time, my grandparents encouraged our participation in the local youth group.

YELLOW LEGAL PAD

About two years after we had gotten connected to the church, the youth director had asked for a high school student to volunteer to preach the message on youth Sunday. No one volunteered. I recalled my time with the church choir and Mr. Spriggs' affirmation, and raised my hand. I knew I was only thirteen, but I already knew that I adored singing from the front of the church. So, what the heck, I knew I could preach.

My youth director gave me a look as if to say, "Are you sure about this?" and to that look I responded with a smile and said, "I think I can do this, Nathan." (Of course his name was 'Nathan'. He even had the tattoo and orange tips in his hair like all the cool youth directors of the late-nineties.)

He nodded with a somewhat more confident smile and agreed, "Ok, Meg's going to bring us the Word."

That night I went and dug out my grandparent's yellow legal pad, a pen, and my teen study bible and went to town.

Though my work was exegetically poor at the time, the message would be over my then favorite Bible verse, Proverbs 17:22, "A cheerful heart is good medicine." My theme would be that the more we intentionally count our blessings, the more blessings we realize that we *actually* have. For the benediction, I felt it was only appropriate for me to sing Bing Crosby's song, *Count Your Blessings*, which I did.

My grandmother bought me a new dress suit to wear for the occasion. It had black pants and a red top with shoulder-pads that should've not been worn by a thirteen-year-old, i.e. I looked older than I was. I think I had the same haircut I have now, a cute lil' brunette bob, and I requested high-heels as to appear taller behind the pulpit. (Because this matters—not! Look at

Joan Of Arc; she was also 5' 3" and did a fine job of inspiring others to act.)

To state that I loved every minute of preaching that Sunday would be like saying the caterpillar loved getting her wings.

I *more* than loved it, I felt as though I was made for it, and it was made for me. After that sermon, I began my route for ordination in the United Methodist Church. My pastor, Royce Riley, and my grandmother began taking me to conferences, seminaries, and connecting me with all sorts of mentors who had similar paths as I desired. This plan and these types of meetings continued throughout high school and college.

Many a moment before taking the mic, my mom would comfort me in the sacristy, "Why are you worried? You know your best work comes when you sing or speak on spiritual things." I have clung to her words over the years.

By the time I graduated college with my Religion and Philosophy degree, I was a certified candidate for ordination and was accepted to two Methodist seminaries.

Yet, I was hesitant to take those next steps.

Somewhere along the way I realized that I had lost myself. I was twenty-two, and while I had been certain for the past eight years of what I was made to do, I was suddenly keenly aware that I had no identity *outside* of the church.

Who was I?

Was I a good friend?

Did I have hobbies? (Does listening to the sermons of others count as a hobby?)

Was I only serving the church because I was so desperate for validation? (And as long as I was a good lil' preaching monkey, they would be happy with me. *Please, someone be happy with me!*)

All of these feelings collided with the issue of a lesbian on our college chapel tech team that led to a demise of some of my relationships—including a romantic one. Apparently, he did not want to date someone who was against his protests against lesbians.

This eruption of feelings (some more repressed than others) led to my complete and utter spiritual burnout my last year of college.

I could not have been *more* done with ministry.

Don't get me wrong, I was not done with Jesus or spirituality. I was just done with church and done with organized religion. For my "big life plan," that meant I was also done with seminary.

My bruised spirit would not let me go to either of the two that had accepted me, and one *even* offered me an amazing financial package. I broke my mentor's and grandparent's hearts with my plans to serve as a teacher in Texas.

Before I could fly south and begin this new chapter (away from the messy and draining world of ministry), there was one last thing I had to do. I had to go on a mission trip to Epworth Children's Home in St. Louis with the college's discipleship team. I might have stopped being a holy-roller, but I was still a cheapskate who had already paid for it. So, I went.

As we arrived on the campus, they asked for three female volunteers who could lead a time of worship for some of the "children." Leah, Megan, and I volunteered. We were then escorted by a security guard. (Yes, you heard me right.) A female police officer led us down this dark, gray, and cold hallway.

She shared that this particular hall was for young women who did not do well in a juvenile detention center. Due to their crimes and behaviors being so foul, they now resided here. I hesitantly smiled and hoped my discomfort would not hinder whatever God had planned for this unexpected time of worship.

The guard punched in the code to the thickest door I had ever seen. As it opened, sounds of chatting teen girls filled the air. I did not think hardened criminals would be talking about prom dresses and contouring, but they were. These young women were articulate, beautiful, and surprisingly hopeful. Never had my expectations for a moment been so far off.

After some high-quality mingling, we awkwardly transitioned into a time of worship through song. We passed out song sheets, and I began to strum and sing the song "Jesus, Lover of My Soul." Everyone sang along, and by the first chorus, I lost myself in the song and closed my eyes in prayer.

As I opened them, I noticed a girl in a pink shirt and a high pony with her eyes tightly shut and tears streaming down her face as she sang. The image pierced my memory. As I looked at her, I heard the Holy Spirit speak within me, (I guess God resorted to words because I was so oblivious to God's voice at that point.)

"I made you for this. I made you for this." (And I guess God repeated it, just to make sure I got the point.)

Once we left Epworth, I vetoed my teaching plans and started applying for church gigs. That same week (I kid you not), one of the pastors called and told me that they were hiring a Minister to Children and Families and since I had interned there for the past four years, they would love for me to "apply." And I served there for over a decade.

SAME WHISPER

While I still went to seminary, fear still owned me regarding my thoughts on becoming an ordained pastor because I wanted a healthy marriage and was utterly disgusted by the suffocating work of the bureaucratic, tactical, business-like work of running a church.

All I wanted to do was to encourage and equip all ages through the written and spoken word, build strong teams, study the brain, and help folks honor how they were wired, so I switched from an MDiv to an MA and paused ordination. I figured I could still preach, without the blame going to me for the company's—I mean, church's—shortcomings since I was not the senior pastor. (Boy, was I wrong there! They'll blame anyone! The stake for burning, unlike our denomination, is all-inclusive.)

Looking back though over this past decade, ministry was *just* as messy for me as a non-ordained minister, if not worse. My job description was less concrete, and I did not have the (mandatory) conference's support to assist me through the conflicts of high-maintenance, emotionally immature parishioners who purely exist to make you fluent in curse words.

I also ran just as many obligatory, tactical committees as the ordained clergy on our staff. While my staff loved me to the greatest of their abilities, ministry is just messy—regardless if you are officially ordained or not. It's messy, awkward and life-sucking in *every* way possible. If one is not in line with his calling as a beloved child of God and living out of his God-given talents, he *won't* last. The local church will eat him alive, as they have done to many ministers before and will continue to do in the years to come.

Our callings as beloved and gifted sustain us. And thankfully I was in line with my vocational calling *enough* to be (mostly) sustainable. I got my fix through lesson planning and empowering our volunteer teams through the written and spoken word.

I just had to supplement my role at the church a bit with "hobbies."

So, what did I do as a hobby while serving as a children's minister?

I worked at *Weight Watchers* where I spoke at weekly meetings. I worked for a civic leadership team where I taught to a group of persons weekly. I said no to God on preaching every Sunday, but like a magnet, I was drawn to opportunities to polish my speaking abilities. I just couldn't stay away from them. They *were* the sacred site of my soul.

And now here I am, embracing it *fully*.

I just packed up my ole' church office and moved into my new one.

Like that thirteen-year-old who scribbled thoughts of Proverbs on a legal pad, I surrender all that I have and give it all I got. I am here, offering up my obsession for creating sacred conversation through books, talks, and a podcast.

I am here, and the same God who whispered, "I made you for this. I made you for this," now nudges, no—imposes upon me, "Are you ready for this? Get ready, and let's do this."

Here I am thankful for the last 15 years of serving children and families in the church and *especially* thankful for how we served kids of troubled homes. I am grateful for this past decade of focusing on becoming a good friend, a good wife, a good mom, and a good "Meg." A "Meg" who *actually* has a healthy life outside of church life. A "Meg" who no longer requires the church's validation for her existence. A "Meg" who is ready for what God has for her next.

As I prepare to leave my post at a church, I feel *so* many feelings, but the loudest feeling is certainty. I feel an undeniable certainty that is found when one's arrived (or returned) to the sacred site of her call.

And in typing 'evolving,' I realize that that's not necessarily the case.

The desires and gifts of the current state of my call have been in me *all along*. Yet, I believe it's *only* when one is living in line with his calling, that the foreshadowing moments of his childhood become apparent in retrospect. These "divine bread-crumbs" as my ole' boss, Dave, would say, that God was leaving to help you discover that which you were made to do, aren't fully appreciated until you park in front of the bakery and smell the scones.

As the great theologian, Howard Thurman taught, "Don't ask what the world needs. Ask what makes you come alive, and go do it. Because what the world needs is people who have come alive."

So how do you know? How do you know if you are doing "the thing" that makes you come most alive? How do you know if you are in line with your calling?

These fascinating questions are exactly what birthed our podcast with the Institute for Discipleship called *The Listening Chair* that explores how vocation, career and God's voice intertwine. Here, my co-host, Miranda Priddy and I interview all kinds of kinds on these questions and the hallowed ground of conversation is insurmountably helpful.

Persons from all over the theological spectrum, in all types of gigs, share tales of following divine nudges to their dream jobs, or infusing their not-so-dreamy job with their callings. Some believe that God called them to their specific *position*. Others believe that God is simply counting on them to serve with certain *talents*. Despite the differing perspectives, there are many commonalities in the interviews that are comparable to Biblical tales of calling.

Like Miriam or Ruth, there was an urgent need to take immediate action and protect another.

Like Moses or Jeremiah, there was an undeniable nudge to move with conviction and courage. The task would be strenuous, but God offered sustenance and direction.

Like Esther or Daniel, there was a realization that an innate quality of theirs could naturally be used to benefit others.

Like Samuel or Mother Mary, there was affirmation from others in answering the call.

Like Mother Mary, there was pure joy felt in living from the sacred site of one's call.

She, as the first disciple of Jesus, sets a mighty example for us.

Did that catch you off guard when I addressed her as that?

It did me as well when she introduced herself as that to me.

CANVAS

During my spiritual burn out period as a college senior, my grandmother took me on a retreat at a Catholic diocese. I arrived there starving for God. On that first night of praying alone in a small chapel, I *feasted*.

A plaque greeted me as I pushed on the door that read, "The Chapel of the First Disciple."

As I entered, the cold tile beneath my feet suddenly warmed due to the bright setting sun through the stain glass. I made my way to the first pew and snuggled in for some prayer. Before I could even close my eyes though, a woman entered my peripheral vision.

To my right was the biggest oil painting I had ever seen. It seriously had to be on a twelve by twelve canvas! Like a Vermeer, there Mary sat facing a window and reading what I assumed was the Holy Scriptures. My awe was momentarily interrupted though as she had a book that had properly been bounded in the style of codex, and this was not historically accurate at all. (Shame on you, Vermeer-wannabe!) I digress.

She was brave and focused.

Oh, is it you? Are you the first disciple of Christ?

I thought as I ignorantly reviewed the call stories of the apostles in the gospels.

Was it not a fisherman or a tax collector?

It was then that the epiphany struck my narrow protestant mind. It was her. Mary of Nazareth *was* the first disciple of Christ, and she had much to teach me at that retreat.

Within the discovery of her calling, teen-mom, Mary experienced a moment of "secret ecstasy" with the Angel Gabriel as described by Tina Beattie. Her call story is such a pivotal moment in our scriptures for in it, "God assures women that he has not forgotten his promise, and that His Word prevails over all the tyranny of history. Man has claimed the right to silence every voice but his, but when God speaks to Mary, He restores the power of speech to women by explicitly excluding man from the event." Even the job of naming the child, which would have been a holy role of the father, was handed over to, the first disciple, Mary.[1]

Through Mary's call story, we are reminded that "[w]e are not made for repetition and conformity. The voice of God calls us out of old patterns of living, and invites us to step into the

---

1   Beattie, Tina. *Rediscovering Mary;* 26.

unknown... Sometimes we must have the courage to not do what is expected of us. We must be willing to break the rules and flaunt the convictions of society, to refuse to collude in systems of oppression and injustice, not in order to conform to the dreary cult of individualism, but in order to forge new paths that others might follow."[2]

While many emotions surrounded Mary's choice to answer the call, it is obvious through her moments of contemplation and action, an insane amount of joy was leading the way. Beattie writes that, "When we discover the biblical Mary, [we see that she was a] free-spirit, and an adventurer[...] She teaches us that discipleship is a constant breaking-free, a passionate openness to the God of life."[3]

The holy and the ordinary, as they often do, were intertwined through Mary's calling. Along with bearing God in human form, she also provided a safe and loving home for Him to grow in, and her love was a key example for His own life mission. As He aged, she encouraged Him of the proper timing of His first miracle, and continued to serve alongside of Him, as an equal to His other disciples.

As He traveled and rumors of His unconventional ways spread, Mary would clarify His work to other members of His family and persuaded them that He was the furthest thing from blaspheme. She evangelized the family, and then joined them as they met with Jesus, "as she is with all those who look for Jesus in bewilderment and questioning."[4]

---

2   Ibid., 30.

3   Ibid., 31.

4   Ibid., 108.

She joined those in their quandaries and in their suffering and this is nowhere more evident than at the cross. While all of the other disciples fled, mother Mary, her sister, John and another apostle, Mary Magdalene, stood by Jesus during this dismal time. This is what Mary desired to do for her son, "She wanted to share his darkness.[…] She could have run away like the other disciples, [...]or prayed behind closed doors, but Mary, the great contemplative, chose to be there in the midst of the violence." Beattie teaches that Mary reveals that stepping, "into suffering beside another person does not diminish the darkness, but it can take away some of the loneliness and the terror of the unknown."[5]

Mary's liberatingly wild and empathetic ways set an example for all of us as we seek to honor our callings. The societal norms were not worth conforming to for her. And neither should they be for us. She submitted to *no one* but God (not even Joseph). She was contemplative but also in on the action. She moved with great conviction and courage. And, like ours can as well, her contributions brought Christ closer to others.

I hear ya. I bypassed the question above, so let's get back to it.

How do you know if you are in line with your vocational calling?

MY TOP FIVE TIPS TO FIND YOUR VOCATIONAL CALLING

1. Don't confuse compliments with calling.

This is in no way news to you, but there are times when our ego leads the way and we serve *not* from an abundance of calling, but

---

5   Ibid., 115.

from desperation of affirmation. In his book, *Let Your Life Speak*, Pastor Parker Palmer tells this grand tale of an opportunity to serve as a college president. As a Quaker, he gathered together with an accountability group and awaited hard questions. When he was asked what about this opportunity made him the most excited, he stated that that would simply be his picture on the front page of the paper announcing his promotion. That was it. It was in that picture and other's reaction to it. His joy was not in the *work*, but in the fame, the recognition, and the affirmation. It was then that he realized that this gig was not in line with his vocational calling; for nothing of the work was truly life-giving to him.

He was living from a place of ego, not a place of calling.

When we are in line with our callings, we honestly don't do it for the compliments. We do it for the insane *joy* of the work. So, while it is nice to receive pats on the back, make sure that is not your sole purpose for serving. Typing from experience, this gets tricky when you are serving in ministry. When the work you are doing is benefiting others, *and* you are complimented left-and-right, this ego-high can sustain you for a little-bit, but not for the long-run. #BurnOut

You will know that you are in line with your vocational calling when the compliments *accompany* a deeply rooted joy and a nearly effortless level of excellence through your work.

2. Seek your time warp.

You will know that you are in line with your vocational calling when time flies and freeze simultaneously, and all you want is more time to do that thing. Is time really freezing/flying by? No, but what's actually happening neurologically when you are doing what you were made to do, or "in the zone"/ "in a flow," is *way* cooler.

(I hear ya. This bit should have been in the "Grit of the Mind" chapter, but you know I'm not a linear thinker, Dear Reader Friend, so it's here. Please direct all complaints to Quoir.com.)

There are conscious and subconscious tasks going on within our brains all of the time. All of the conscious "stuff" has to go through a bottleneck called the thalamus. Yep, any sound, sight, thought, or sensation goes through here. Each of these is known as a "bit," and the limit of the capacity of the thalamus is 126 bits per second. This is why your kid talking to you while you are ordering at *Sonic* is beyond annoying.

Now, what happens when we are carrying out a task that's in line with our passions and talents ("in a flow state"/ "in the zone") is the opposite of the sensory overload that is ordering a *Wacky Pack* with a wailing wacky toddler in the back seat. As brain-surgeon, Dr. Allan Hamilton, explains, "as a challenge calls on more of our [rewarding] skills, we bring a greater focus on it. More and more sensory information is pulled into perform-ing the task and less conscious processing is available for other things. Thanks to the bottleneck [thalamus], we lose awareness of what is going on around us, of how time is moving, and even of our own thought processes. The task literally pulls so much current, so much sensory "juice," that we lose our self-awareness and we *become* the task. We may refer to this state of mind as "being in the zone," but what we actually are alluding to is that so much of our focus is brought to bear on our objective that our skills, our motor abilities, all are deferred to subconscious control."[6]

Did I just blow your mind? (I mean, your thalamus?)

3. Observe your effortless grit.

When you are in line with your vocational calling, you naturally perform at a higher quality and are sustained through *even* the hardest of days.

This is best illustrated in the story by the comedian, Mindy Kaling, and the birth (pun intended) of her show, "The Mindy Project."

Kaling based this show on her Mom who was an OB/GYN. Her show got picked up by FOX on the same day that her mom passed from pancreatic cancer. To say Kaling was close with her mom is the understatement of the century. She considered her a soul-mate. While the grief was insurmountable, Kaling honored her mom's legacy in doing what she was made to do and created an amazing sitcom.

Even through this gut-wrenchingly difficult time, her call sustained her with joy, grit, and with the nearly effortless ability to write, act, direct, and produce well.

4. See your present steps by surrendering to your future vision.

Sometimes, when awakening us to our callings, the Holy Spirit might provide us with a vision that depicts our life in the future. One might receive a big picture dream of his ideal workspace, or end goal, but then (what seems like) nothing else. This leaves much to be desired in regards to one's first step toward that vision.

---

6   Hamilton; *The Source of Flow*, 56-60.

You must surrender to this vision and *fully* trust it in order to see the steps to actualizing it. Perhaps your first step is direct messaging a master in the field on *Twitter*. This step leads to a *Zoom* session. During that zoom session you're given an application for an internship, which evolves into the gig of your vision from years prior.

The *Twitter* message and the *Zoom* chat wouldn't have been if you hadn't surrendered and *trusted* the vocational vision that God placed on your heart. Even if you're told that the dream-job of your vision doesn't exist, or you yourself don't fully understand it. Surrender to it. Trust it.

Another way to look at this is through Psalm 119:105, "Thy word is a lamp unto my feet, and a light unto my path."

My friend, Karen, unpacks this verse through a story on a camping trip.

She shares on how one night, in a deep dark hour, she had to use the restroom. She wrestled out of her tent, and with a flashlight, walked into the black abyss. As she shined the light ahead of her, she could see into the distance. As she shined the light downward, she could watch where her feet were landing as to not trip, but she couldn't see both the distance and her feet simultaneously.

This psalm came to her mind as she searched for the outhouse. It reminded her of how God is faithful in shedding light on both our present and our future.

As she shared this with me, I was reminded of one's vocational journey. While seeking our callings, God will provide the clarity we need for each step. And if you are like me and God provides you with a vision before the specific first steps, remember to surrender to the future vision in order to see the steps of the present.

5. One Calling, Different Gigs

My good ole' campus minister, Rev. Ashlee Alley Crawford used to teach us to consider our life-callings as life mission statements. Under the "umbrellas" of these statements we would hold different positions that aim for the same mission and use similar talents. This was so refreshing and comforting to hear, seeing as how studies suggest that millennials will have many more jobs in their lifetime than their boomer parents. (And Gen Zs will all be four-hundred-pound solopreneurs who only work three-months out of the year from their home offices.)

Think about it. One's life mission statement could be, "I will take medical care to those who struggle to get it." This person could at first be a certified doula in Dallas for low-income moms, later become a missionary nurse who serves in orphanages in Matamoros, and then be a instructor at the University of Cambridge who trains the next generation to live out a similar mission. This person will be living out of the same mission statement through an ever-evolving list of positions in which she is using similar talents and interests.

Or to think even broader, one's vision statement could be, "I was made to challenge the process." This person could then serve as a teacher, a pastor, a counselor, or a politician. Or another example, say someone serves as a middle school class officer's sponsor, then a life-coach and then founds a civic leadership program with the mission statement of "I was made to nurture leaders." And lastly, someone could live out of the mission statement of, "I was made to have tough conversations with grace." She works for an airline in the department that deals with folks who lose their luggage or miss their flights, then she collects late payments at a church pre-school, then she becomes a mortician and enjoys writing the eulogies with families.

See?

One calling, *many* different gigs.

When you are seeking to live from that sacred site which is your vocational calling, don't confuse compliments *with* your calling, seek your time warp, observe your effortless grit, see your present steps by surrendering to your future vision, and give yourself permission to have a strand of different, evolving gigs under a similar life mission statement.

VOS AUTEM SANCTUM TUU

May these five tips guide you in the awareness of your calling and as your talents nurture others, may you not forget to nurture *yourself.* In the rush of your career, don't miss out on what matters most in life. Although it may be tempting, don't rely on the validation of others. True validation comes from within and you are *already* enough. As you house the Holy, you already possess enough grace for every wound and enough grit for every goal.

You, yes, *all of you*, are your own sanctuary.

You are safe, you are loved, and you *so* got this.

You are your own sanctuary.

Your being houses the Holy.
Grit and grace come from within,
regardless of the choices of others.

234

Your body is beautiful;
a gift that should be cared for,
trusted, and never feared.

Your mind is uniquely yours.
While it is ever-expanding,
you call the shots on its focus,
stillness, and creativity.

Your emotions are all necessary
and should be embraced.

Your spirit was made for
a relationship with God and others.

Your soul holds a sacred site
from which you serve with your talents.

AS YOU FORGE ONWARD AS YOUR OWN SANCTUARY, ASK YOURSELF:

1. In reflecting on your childhood, what foreshadowing breadcrumbs to your vocational calling do you see? What words were used to describe younger you? What were your favorite toys? Who did you look up to? What were some of your first talents others saw?

2. If you are seeking your vocational calling, what do you want the Holy Spirit to whisper to or impose upon you? Of the five tips, which one(s) rang the truest for you? Which one(s) led to the most curiosity? With which one(s) did you disagree? Why?

3. Through Mary's call story we are reminded that, "We are not made for repetition and conformity. The voice of God calls us out of old patterns of living, and invites us to step into the unknown[...] Sometimes we must have the courage to *not do* what is expected of us." Are there expectations of others that are preventing you from following your vocational calling? If so, write a prayer below to navigate this as you answer the call. If this is not the case, for *what* do you need courage in answering your call?

Bibliography

1. Barclay, William. *The Daily Bible Study Series: The Gospel of Matthew Vol. II*. Philadelphia : Saint Andrews Press, 1976.

2. Beattie, Tina. *Rediscovering Mary: Insights from the Gospels* . Liguori: Triumph Books, 1995.

3. Bell, Rob ,Don Goldan. *Jesus Wants to Save Christians: A Manifesto for the Church in Exile*. Grand Rapids: Zondervan, 2008.

4. Brown, Lachlan. "Hackspirit.com ." *Hackspirit.com* . December 5 , 2017. https://hackspirit.com/pit-stomach-actually-second-brain-heres-heal/ (accessed August 19, 2018).

5. Bryson, Tina Payne, and Dan Siegal. *The Yes Brain*. New York: Bantum, 2018.

6. Darling, Daniel. "Christianity Today International." *Christianity Today. com*. October 2015. https://www.christianitytoday.com/pastors/2015/october-web-exclusives/essential-art-of-forgiveness-in-ministry.html (accessed October 4, 2018).

7. Doidge, Norman. *The Brain That Changes Itself*. London: Penguin, 2007.

8. Guttmacher Institute. "Trends in Premarital Sex in the United States, 1954-2003." *US National Library of Medicine*, Public Health Rep. (2007 Jan-Feb) :73-8. https://www.ncbi.nlm.nih.gov/pubmed/17236611 (accessed March 12, 2019).

9. Gilbert, Elizabeth. *Committed; A Skeptic Makes Peace with Marriage Penguin Group*. New York City: The Penguin Group, 2010.

10. Grenz, Stanley J. *Theology for the Community of God*. Cambridge: Broadman & Holman , 1994.

11. Hamilton, Allan. "The Source of Flow and The Battle of the Bottleneck." *Spirituality and Health*, 2018: 56-60.

12. Hayward, David. *The Liberation of Sophia*. David Hayward, *2014.*

13. Killingsworth, Matt. "TedSummaries.com ." *TedSummaries.com.* October 19, 2014. https://tedsummaries.com/2014/10/19/matt-killingsworth-want-to-be-happier-stay-in-the-moment/ (accessed November 13, 2018).

14. Koulopoulos, Thomas. *INC.com.* July 23, 2017. https://www.inc.com/thomas-koulopoulos/according-to-science-this-5-second-rule-will-make-.html (accessed september 4, 2018).

15. McCleneghan, Bromleigh. *Good Christian Sex: Why Chastity Isn't the Only Option--and Other Things the Bible Says About Sex.* New York City: HarperOne, 2016.

16. McGowan, Kathleen. *The Source of Miracles: 7 Steps to Transforming Your Life Through The Lord's Prayer.* New York City: Touchstone , 2009.

17. Newell, J. Philip. *Christt of the Celts: The Healing of Creation* . San Fransico: Jossey Bass, 2008.

18. Nouwen, Henri. *The Return of the Prodigal Son: A Story of Homecoming.* New York City : Doubleday, 1994.

19. Norton, Joan and Maragaret Starbird. *14 Steps to Awaken the Sacred Feminine.* Rockchester: Bear & Company, 2009.

20. Ph.D., Edward A. Selby. "Rumination: Probem Solving Gone Wrong ." *Psychology today* . february 10, 2010. https://www.psychologytoday.com/us/blog/overcoming-self-sabotage/201002/rumination-problem-solving-gone-wrong (accessed September 13, 2018).

21. Rapura, Ash. "Ruby Wax in conversation with a Neuroscientist, a Monk & Louise Chunn". Interviewed by Louise Chunn. *Penguin UK.* February 19, 2018.

22. Seppala, Emma. "The Loneliness Paradoxes." *Spirituality and Health*, 2018 : 100-101.

23. Siegel, Dan and David Rock. *Healthy Mind Platter.* 2011. http://www. drdansiegel.com/resources/healthy_mind_platter/ (accessed September 4, 2018).

24. Stevenson-Moessner, Jeanne. *A Primer in Pastoral Care* . Minneapolis : Augsburg Fortress , 2005.

25. Sullivan, James. *The Good Listener* . Notre Dame: Ave Maria , 2000.

26. Wax, Ruby. *How To Be Human, the Manual.* Great Brittan : Penguin Life, 2017.

27. Sullivan Bob, and Hugh Thompson. "Brain Interrupted" New York Times. (2013 May): https://www.nytimes.com/2013/05/05/opinion/ sunday/a-focus-on-distraction.html.

28. Whitaker, Todd. *Shifting the Monkey.* Bloomington: Triple Nickel Press, 2012.

29. Willard, Dallas. *Renovation of the Heart: Putting on the Character of Christ.* Colorado Springs: NavPress , 2002.

30. Winner, Lauren. *Real Sex: The Naked Truth About Chasitity* . Grand Rapids: BrazosPress, 2005.

31. Yotopoulos, Amy. "Three Reasons Why People Don't Volunteer and What Can be Done About It." The Sightlines Project. http://longevity. stanford.edu/three-reasons-why-people-dont-volunteer-and-what-can-be-done-about-it/.

For more information about Meggie Lee Calvin
or to contact her for speaking engagements,
please visit *www.MegCalvin.com*

Many voices. One message.

Quoir is a boutique publisher
with a singular message: *Christ is all.*
Venture beyond your boundaries to discover Christ
in ways you never thought possible.

For more information, please visit
www.quoir.com